John Hartson's
CELTIC DREAM TEAM

John Hartson's CELTIC DREAM TEAM

JOHN HARTSON

WITH IAIN KING

BLACK & WHITE PUBLISHING

First published 2012
by Black & White Publishing Ltd
29 Ocean Drive, Edinburgh EH6 6JL

1 3 5 7 9 10 8 6 4 2   12 13 14 15

ISBN: 978 1 84502 499 4

A CIP catalogue record for this book is available from the British Library.

Typeset by Iolaire Typesetting, Newtonmore
Printed and bound by MPG Books Ltd, Bodmin, Cornwall

DEDICATIONS

JOHN HARTSON

This book is dedicated to the Lisbon Lions, the team who put Celtic firmly on the map. Once I knew the history the Lions captivated me and I feel humbled that I wore the same shirt they did. They are legends in my eyes.

I also want to take this chance to thank every Celtic fan who thought of me and sent me a message when I was at death's door. You helped to bring me back from the brink. I am proud to be a part of the Celtic family. Martin O'Neill always told me to make Paradise my home as a footballer – and I did.

IAIN KING

The idea to embark on this project was born in the wake of the death of my mum, Leila King. This book and the fun I have had with big bad John in the writing of it has helped me through a difficult year.

I'd like to dedicate the book to my mum and her memory, she always believed in me with all her heart and her pride in my achievements as a journalist made every sacrifice I have made for the job worthwhile. Rest in peace, Ma. Always. Always.

CONTENTS

FOREWORD
BY NEIL LENNON
Manager, Celtic Football Club

'Hospital spokesmen in Swansea have confirmed that John Hartson, the former Celtic and Wales footballer, has testicular cancer and that it has spread to his brain.'

I heard that news on the radio driving into the Celtic training ground and I had to pull the car over to the side of the road. I sat there and burst into tears. It had come out of the blue and I could not believe this was happening to someone so close to me. I got straight on the phone to Jackie McNamara, who was John's roommate through all his years at the club. We were both stunned and I rushed to speak to John's father Cyril and his wife Sarah, and we all just started praying.

For anyone to come through what John did is something that I now consider to be a miracle. He dropped six and a half stones in weight and looking at him walking on the zimmer when he came out of hospital broke my heart. It didn't suit him being that thin, he just wasn't big bad John. Now I see him and he's back to this huge presence, he's his big jovial self in a room again and I just thank God he's here. It's great to see. I mean, he survived fourteen major operations and sixty-seven sessions of chemotherapy – it's astonishing what he has come through. The wounds he now carries are constant reminders, the battering his body has taken is harrowing – but he withstood it.

Now my team has had to cope with another of our own, Stiliyan Petrov, facing the same sort of battle with leukaemia and the news he was in remission was wonderful to hear too. I think that team has a special bond, the Seville boys. We were all around the same age, apart from Stan, who was the youngest. I played with some good teams but that Celtic group that Martin O'Neill assembled had a lot of hard bastards in it. By that I mean mentally strong individuals who you could count on when the chips were down. We had some great nights out together but we didn't suffer fools gladly either if we felt we had a slacker in our midst. And maybe at that time in our careers guys like me and John needed a manager like Martin O'Neill. We were seasoned pros by then and in the team talks he didn't really need to say that much. We all knew what was at stake and what was in front of us.

I had worked with Martin at Leicester City from the age of twenty-four and as I got older I knew where he was coming from. It didn't stop the likes of John and me having barneys with him, right enough! We never won those arguments because when Martin lost it – as he did on a famous occasion when John threw sandwiches about the Hampden dressing room after being subbed – then it was memorable. Stand back.

John arrived at the club a year after me, and Henrik Larsson and Chris Sutton had just scored sixty-six goals between them the season before. They were some partnership. The big man, though, was never short of confidence in his own ability and he was bang in form for Coventry City at the time. I remember just before our interest in him became public he had scored two for them at Old Trafford when Andy Goram was on loan and in goal for Manchester United. Wherever Harts went he had faith in what he could do as a striker, and that was one of the character traits that I loved about him.

I remember playing against him when I was at Leicester City and he was at Arsenal. He was this hulking nineteen-year-old striker and even though we had big boys at the back he was rag-dolling them around the place. He was awesome alongside Dennis Bergkamp and they ran amok as they beat us 2-0. Even at that age you could tell he was a quality player.

Martin O'Neill always liked a big centre-forward and I always felt that he had this fear inside of him of something happening to Sutty, who was such a pivotal part of our team. When we got John he knew he had a ready-made replacement or he could play the two of them together if needed. In the end, John had a phenomenal time at the club and his goalscoring record here of those 110 strikes and almost a goal every two games stands up there with the best of them. He was a twenty-goals-a-season man but I agree with what he states in the pages you are about to read – he could have scored even MORE for Celtic.

Everyone thinks of John Hartson as this big battering ram but he had great feet for such a big man and he had a terrific touch and an appreciation of where people were about him. We all know he wasn't the most mobile of footballers, but he compensated for that in so many other ways. His game intelligence was very good and he was one of the best headers of a ball I have ever seen. He was fantastic, he could hold people off and still get thumping headers in, which is a talent in itself. He was an excellent technician as a striker, he was just a top player.

John has become a Celtic man, although to his credit he never claims to have been born one, but he has become one. He is very fondly thought of at this club and rightly so. He scored in big games, he had the mentality to do that and, let's be honest, that always helps you win over the fans. I think he will always treasure the five years we had together at Celtic. It was a golden time for so many of us in our careers. Like everyone who supports Celtic, the goal against Liverpool at Anfield in the UEFA Cup on the run to Seville will always stick in my mind. He played this great one-two with Henrik, shifted his feet round a tackle and BANG! It just flew past Jerzy Dudek from twenty-five yards and we were on our way to the semi-final. You just don't forget nights – or goals – like that.

Just look at his contribution on that run, holding the guy off and smashing the ball low into the corner away to Celta Vigo. It was a crying shame he missed the final through injury but he also scored nine Old Firm goals which, as I say, always helps you win a place in the hearts of the Hoops fans! He was a remarkable specimen as a footballer, you just used to look at him sometimes and wonder how the hell he was going to get around the pitch. Then the cross would come in and he would be planted there in the middle of the goal to hold off a big bruiser of a centre-half and power home the header. Nothing fazed him as a player. He had this mentality that if he missed a chance then he would score the next one. He carried that confidence inside himself.

He cost over £20 million in transfer fees throughout his career and I think people forget that when Harry Redknapp bought John, West Ham United were really struggling in the Premiership. Harry went and got John, Paul Kitson and Steve Lomas, who is now the St Johnstone manager with me in the SPL, and those three signings kept them up. That's the impact John could have, so we knew what we were getting when he came to Celtic and I think he left the club at the right time too, which is important. He left having scored a goal that won the league against Hearts and, like me when I went to Nottingham Forest towards the end of my playing days, he discovered the same buzz isn't there when you leave a club like Celtic.

The thing I love about Harts is that he could make me look good at pre-season! He actually used to go to the gym and when no-one was looking he would pour a bottle of water over himself to make it look like he had been sweating in case Martin walked past. Priceless!

When Gordon Strachan arrived the emphasis on the fitness of the players was intensified and that wasn't great for the big man. There's this running drill called the Bleep Test and John hated it. So it was the start of the week and we knew the Bleep was coming and Harts tells the gaffer his hamstring is hellishly tight and he just can't do it. We all slog through it and come Friday we were down to train at Celtic Park.

Funnily enough, big John declared himself fit for the Saturday match on the Thursday and he was buzzing and looking forward to our normal game of Young v Old, or whatever was in store on the Friday. Anyway, we got there and Gordon said to him, 'How are you feeling, John?'

He replied, 'Great, boss. I feel magnificent.'

Gordon said, 'That's great news. You boys, turn right and enjoy your game. John, you turn left, the Bleep Test is set up behind the goal at the far end.'

He hadn't got away with it! Gordon was wise to him and he had to go through it anyway. I asked John how it went afterwards and he said the groundsman beat him. Seriously, though, when he trained he trained well and in that season on the road to Seville he was at his peak. He feared no-one.

We had a brilliant man-manager when John checked into Celtic, the sort of man-manager he needed at a stage of his career when he had seen four moves collapse on him because of failed medicals. The club was flying, and I think John loved being a part of that group of players. It's an interesting one to ponder why big John ended up falling in love with Celtic when he had bounced around a few clubs in England, scoring goals wherever he went. I just think he was Welsh, a Celt, he had a working-class background and this club was a great fit for him. The whole philosophy of the club appeals to people like John and me, who I see as down-to-earth guys. John can sit in a pub anywhere and talk football with people from any walk of life.

He got Celtic, that's the way I would describe it. And it pleases me to see the high regard he is now held in by the Celtic family – because he earned it.

Neil Lennon
Lennoxtown
September 2012

INTRODUCTION

THE CELTIC DRAGON

When I was at my lowest ebb, when I was dying, I had the Celtic family at my bedside.

The 60,000 fans who pack Paradise weren't there in person, they couldn't be, but I could genuinely feel their spirit as I teetered on the brink. I know deep down now that during that long, wretched battle with cancer there was a time when I was gone, when I was dead.

My own family brought me back from that darkest of places but so too did the love of all the people who sent me messages when I was hooked up to all those machines, breathing through a ventiliator and clinging onto this world for dear life.

I had fourteen major operations, sixty-seven sessions of chemotherapy, but still every day of that journey back from the dead the nurses would bring me a box of cards and messages. The hospital in Swansea had never seen anything like the mail, the flowers, the telegrams that I got, and 95 per cent of it was from Celtic fans.

Sure, my old club, Arsenal, remembered me and prayed for me, so did all my former clubs and so did the fans of my two bitterest rivals as a football man and a football fan, Rangers and Cardiff City. That meant a lot.

These days looking at my body is like reading some battered road map that tells you the hellish journey I have been through. The dents in my head from the two brain operations that kept me out of the morgue, the fourteen-inch scars on my back where they got into my lungs to save me. I look like a Samurai has attacked me.

Those wounds tell you the story of a guy who had a lump on his testicles for FOUR YEARS and didn't have the maturity to face up to what he knew was cancer. Do you know something, I'd discovered it first in my Celtic days and I tried to ignore it.

But in those quiet moments, the private times when it's just you and your thoughts swirling around, I had this picture in my head. It was of me walking into a doctor's room, or a hospital, and them telling me exactly what I heard one fateful afternoon in Swansea. I foresaw it, I knew that I had cancer.

I still wince when I look back on the worst days of my life, to the blinding headache that went on for days, when nothing could stop the pain. I felt so bad I asked my sister to take me to hospital. The cancer was right on top of me then and those next six weeks were a blur.

I was all over the place then, and I can remember at one point ripping the tubes out of my body and staggering around the room with nurses trying to hold me down. I didn't want to die but the pain was too much. If I was seventy-five, I'd have said, 'God, take me.' But I was thirty-four and I had Sarah, the kids and my family to live for.

There's something that chills me even yet when I think back to those awful days. When I was rushed into hospital it was a ten-minute ambulance ride to the Neurology Unit in Swansea; it's moved to Cardiff now. If it had been Cardiff back then I'd be dead. That's not me being dramatic for the sake of a book, that's just me telling the truth. Yet after all the ravages that cancer left on me, those scars are not what I choose to see first. First I look at my tattoos.

I have the Celtic badge, 'You'll Never Walk Alone' etched underneath it and the number 110, signifying the amount of goals I scored for the club, on my body. I am proud of every one of them. Right from the start at the Hoops I knew I could never be as good a player as Henrik Larsson was, I was playing with greatness but I thought my chance for a place in the history books at Celtic Park was to score 100 goals for the club. I did it and I am immensely satisfied with that. I will be able to take that to my deathbed, as I will my tattoos. Some people don't like them but I love them and all of mine mean something – the Celtic ones, all my kids' names, the Welsh dragon on my leg, my tiger, which is a sign of strength to mark my recovery. My Celtic tattoos are proof of what this great club means to me.

I understand the cynicism when you speak of the power of people's thoughts dragging you out of the abyss, but all I would say is that I have been there. My dad was always showing me the messages of support from the Celtic fans and telling me they were all willing me to beat this. It meant the world to me. The world of football came together to pull for me the way they did when the Bolton midfielder Fabrice Muamba collapsed on the pitch with heart failure that nightmarish day against Spurs.

My fight was against the cancer that had riddled my body and, as people wondered if I could make it, the only news they could get were the nuggets of information the doctors would release in their statements. There was a risk of infection and I was holed up in there all alone, fighting for my life. When I came to, though, every letter I had from the Celtic family gave me a little ounce more of inspiration. Young children were in school writing letters to me and telling me I was their hero.

Then I would get pictures from their mums and dads showing me as this big strapping Celtic star glowing with health and at the peak of his powers, telling me that I could get back to that one day. I didn't think so – as far as I was concerned I had been reduced to a skeleton in hospital and I was scared stiff when I looked at my reflection in the mirror.

Yet they all believed in me at the time when I needed them most, and you can't quantify the debt that I owe to the Celtic supporters. They even put a book together for me that has something like 7,000 signatures in it and I read every single personal message in there. They meant so much to me. I firmly believe now that when I was in dire straits, in the most desperate trouble of my life, that their faith in me helped me pulled me back from checking out for good. Simple as that. I lost about six and a half stone in all and I came out needing a zimmer to walk. I was a shadow of myself but every step I took on that zimmer I would think of sticking around for Sarah and my kids then I'd remember the way I'd been when I was healthy and scoring goals for Celtic. Then I'd look at the goodwill messages and think I couldn't give up now and let them all down.

Celtic has come to mean so much to me now. It's such a massive club. I had played for Arsenal in two European finals before I arrived in Scotland and I felt the size of that football club. We took 35,000 fans to the Parc des Princes for the 1995 Cup Winners' Cup final against Real Zaragoza when we lost 2-1 and my goal wasn't enough to save us. I knew what it was like to play for big clubs.

Yet nothing can prepare you for the size of Celtic Football Club. In my eyes, they are a true world brand in football. They have a fan base that you wouldn't believe. I'll never forget the day that I signed, there were thousands outside the ground all clapping and singing and cheering. It was unreal.

When you sign for a club down south – even one of the big ones like Arsenal or West Ham United – you sign the forms in the boardroom and when you come out there might be six or seven punters waiting for an autograph who have heard a whisper about the deal on the radio.

When I joined up for my first Welsh international squad after I signed for Celtic, the boys asked me to describe what it was like. I told them the home games were like playing an international. That was the best comparison I could give them.

No disrespect, but 99 times out of 100 we would beat teams like Dunfermline at home and seven or eight times out of ten I knew I would score because we created so many chances. When you play for Celtic at home, it's like one big party. It started with the 'Fields of Athenry' and all the songs I grew to love and the atmosphere just built until the kick-off, it was like a carnival every time we played for Celtic. The fans make that place so special and you just can't help but absorb it all.

Those five years I spent in Paradise were the best of my football career. I came into a side that already had Henrik

Larsson and Chris Sutton in it and people say I must have been daunted. Maybe a little, but why live in fear? I would learn later in my life there were bigger, scarier battles to fight than the one I had for a starting slot at Celtic.

My first goals there came on Saturday, October 20, 2001 and they will live with me until the day I die. People look back now and think that I waited a long time to get the breakthrough. It was, after all, ten games until I got my first goal. I think that's a misleading picture, though, because I only started three of those ten matches and I was finding my feet. I was coming off the bench, and when you are a striker it's very difficult to do that and make an impact.

It wasn't haunting me, breaking my duck, but I'd be lying if I didn't say that I knew in the appearances column it said ten and in the goals column there was a big fat zero! It was starting to bother me slightly, and then came that Dundee United match. I'll always remember that Dundee United were trying to play a high line up the pitch to try and frustrate us, catch us offside. They reckoned without the magician that was Lubo Moravčik, though, and he slid in a terrific ball to put me clean through. He was a genius, Lubo, and the pace of the ball was perfect for me. I remember running through and I was just thinking, 'Don't miss, don't miss, don't miss.' There were 60,000 looking down on me and I felt this was the first real chance I'd had in that opening spell at the club. I was one-on-one with the goalkeeper and I slotted it with the outside of my right foot inside the far corner. It was an amazing feeling and I think the fans were desperate for me to score that day, they could sense my frustration.

I was trying so hard for them and, looking back, I should have just settled down and trusted in my ability. My record spoke for itself. I had always scored goals at Arsenal, West Ham and Wimbledon. It wasn't an issue, but the truth is Celtic meant so much to me. I was born to score goals, had loved the feeling since I was six years old, but getting off the mark still felt like a massive weight had been lifted off my shoulders. One soon became three, a tap-in then I cashed in after a mistake from their centre-half, we won 5-1 and I had my hat-trick.

I still have all my hat-trick balls, you know. I only scored trebles for West Ham and Celtic and those match balls are in my mum and dad's converted loft where a lot of my souvenirs from my career also rest. I should get it out one day and show it all to my son Joni, but the truth is that so far he hasn't bloody asked!

In my office at home I have just three keepsakes. I could have shirts from all the great players I played against all over the house but after all I have been through I would rather have pictures of my kids hanging on the walls. I have a Welsh international shirt signed by the likes of Aaron Ramsey and Gareth Bale – they sent that to the hospital when I was clinging on in there and, when I came to, it meant the world to see it. I also have a Wales rugby jersey of Gareth Edwards with number 9 on the back. He was my hero and in my opinion one of the greatest rugby players who ever lived. And from me? It's a picture I had commissioned in Glasgow of me scoring for Celtic against Liverpool. It cost me a bit of dough but that was the goal of my life. It's worth it. I think those three choices tell you something about me as a person. I could have a shrine to my career all around the house but the office is my own little space where I go to think and clear my head and those memories stay in there.

I have a great friend in my life, James Kean, a self-made construction tycoon in East Kilbride who played for Ayr United and Clyde. He's a great football guy, Keany, he was best pals with the late, great Tommy Burns and he has been friends with current Rangers manager Ally McCoist since they were kids. Keany loves the game and has some brilliant jerseys and stuff, but it's all down-stairs in his bar where the boys have a pint and watch games on the TV. It's not on show in the house – his kids are. Like mine.

Listen, though, after that first hat-trick for Celtic I never stopped scoring for the club. I was addicted to the feeling, to be honest. Loved it. The first season I scored twenty-five, the second season I got twenty-three, the third season I had two back operations and hit twelve before Christmas, the fourth season Henrik Larsson had left and I took on the mantle of responsibility and hit thirty goals and my last season I got twenty and was joint top-scorer with Maciej Zurawski.

That's how my 110 was pieced together, that was my Celtic record and I am proud of it, my best in the English Premiership had been twenty-four at West Ham and I came to Scotland with that twenty landmark in my mind each season. I feel as a striker with the Old Firm you should be scoring at least twenty a season because you are playing with the best players and you are getting the most chances. For four out of my five years in the Hoops I did that, and only the surgeon's knife stopped me from making it five out of five. I will always look at the fact that I stayed in the side and that Martin O'Neill adapted

Chris Sutton's position to midfield or centre-half to accommodate me as one of the biggest compliments I was ever paid as a footballer.

That first season at Celtic, though, I had to be patient. Three days after that first hat-trick for the Hoops we went out to Norway to play Rosenborg in the Champions League and I was on the bench. That was Martin, he had a plan in his mind and me landing with the match ball on the Saturday wasn't going to change it one little bit. I was a sub, I only got on for the last twelve minutes and Harald Brattbakk – who'd scored one of the goals for Celtic against St Johnstone that stopped ten-in-a-row for Rangers in 1998 – had a dream night, as we lost 2-0. I knew for sure now I was at a big club with a single-minded gaffer, I had just scored three and I was left out.

The press tried to get me to bite on a story afterwards and voice my dissatisfaction to give them a back-page headline, but I knew better than that. I said the right things because deep down I realised that I was still bedding into the club. By the next time we played away in Europe, in the Mestalla against Valencia, I was in the starting line-up when we lost 1-0 and by and large when it mattered on the continent I was a pick from then on in.

And those nights came to mean the world to me. I treasure the goals I scored away in Europe for Celtic – in Lyon, in Spain at Celta Vigo, against my boyhood heroes Liverpool at Anfield, in front of 100,000 fans against Barcelona in the Nou Camp. Those were big goals, and as far as I am concerned, big players score big goals. You make a difference when it matters. For a Celtic striker that means in Europe or against Rangers, even though I would never have the lack of respect there is in that theory that any old player could score for Celtic against Hibs or Dunfermline. That's just bollocks.

Still, there was an extra edge required to net in Europe or in the Old Firm games and I scored nine times against Rangers – it should have been eleven, but two of those were disallowed for nothing. It was a conspiracy! Seriously, there was so much to savour, highs and lows. I scored a Cup final goal against Rangers at Hampden but we lost that Scottish Cup final 3-2 and I also missed a last-gasp penalty in a League Cup final defeat. This club puts you in situations that can rip your emotions to shreds. I can't explain adequately the feeling of scoring those nine goals against Rangers. Last night people will have gone to bed in Glasgow and if you're a Celtic fan, at some point in your life if you don't admit you've woken up thinking you scored the winner against them during the night, then you're a liar! It is the stuff of dreams and I scored in four consecutive Old Firm derbies, so imagine that. They were ready to give me the keys to one half of the city. The green and white half. It was such a joy and inside it wasn't bitterness or hatred driving me on, but there was a sense of revenge in there. I scored a late goal against them in a Scottish Cup quarter-final just after I'd signed a new contract and ran away thinking I was worth it!

When I went to Rangers in August 2000 I walked down the track at Ibrox with the media in tow and I was there with every intention of signing for the club. The Rangers chairman, Sir David Murray, had flown me there on his private jet from the Welsh camp, Mark Hughes had given me permission to travel and I thought I was set for a life-changing move. Instead, on the day they signed Ronald de Boer for £4.5 million, they failed me on the medical and they hung me out to dry. I have had to live with the fall-out of that and get over it. Once I became a Celtic player you'd better believe there was an extra determination within me to show Rangers what they had let go and what they had missed out on. Anyone with a little bit of pride and desire in their DNA, and I had plenty of both, would have felt the same way. It had nothing to do with religion or anything else – to think I hate Rangers is nonsense. I'm John Hartson from Swansea. I wasn't born into that side of it. I wouldn't patronise people and pretend I was.

I would have signed there and then for Rangers, I won't lie about that, but after they dumped me they didn't really care what happened to my career, what the consequences of that decision would be for me. Truth is, I think they couldn't have cared less whether I played football again.

That was the fourth medical I had failed and I had to show a real inner desire to recover from that decision. It was a body blow for me. I was publicly jettisoned and every goal against the team who turned me down after that meant so much more. I also felt I was vindicating Martin O'Neill, showing the world that he was right and Rangers were wrong. I hope that gave the gaffer a lot of satisfaction. He had faith in me, he proved that they had made a big mistake and I think I paid him back. The irony is that if you look at the traditional Celtic strikers then I was more suited to being a Rangers player.

When I went for my medical I was sat in the dressing room and Andrei Kanchelskis, Jorg Albertz and John Brown were all in there. I have become good friends with 'Bomber' Brown and he said to me back then, 'This is brilliant, I'm delighted you are coming here. You are exactly what we need.' All the players were overjoyed I was on the way in and I was really excited by their reaction – then it was all pulled away from me. They had looked for a successor to Mark Hateley and they felt that in me they had found one at last.

Like Hateley, I was an old-fashioned centre-forward. If we weren't scoring we'd be knocking them back for Henrik Larsson or, in his case, the great Ally McCoist. I was more of a Hateley figure and I would have suited Rangers and the way they played. I'll never forget Barry Ferguson laughing to me: 'I can't believe that wee bastard Advocaat never signed you.' And I feel there is respect there from the Rangers fans, a lot of my Glasgow friends now are Rangers-minded.

I think the manager has the last word in circumstances like that. He had to respect what the doctor was telling him but he had the last word. This big Dutch doc Gert Jan Goudswaard said my knee was dodgy and that Rangers shouldn't do it and Dick took his word for it. I have to respect that. Martin O'Neill, though, didn't do that. He threw all that away and he said he was signing me because he knew you could scan a lot of players and their knee wouldn't show up 100 per cent perfect. Martin said he trusted in me as a player and I always felt I owed him for that and I set about paying him back over those five years at Celtic.

Martin did a foreword for my autobiography, and that meant the world to me. He cracked a few jokes and he spoke highly of me and that meant so much. I could have left Celtic for the likes of Middlesbrough when they were cash-rich under Steve McClaren in the Premiership. Always in my head, though, was my debt to Martin and that target of 100 goals. It became an obsession of mine. I left with a year left on my contract – who knows what total it could have been. I have my 110, though, and I am proud of that.

I was thirty-one when I left Celtic and my personal life with my divorce was at a low ebb. On the field we were champions and I had just finished top goalscorer. Listen, though, you make decisions on what is happening in your life at the time and I made my call.

I will always carry one regret, though, and that was not getting the chance to say a proper farewell to the fans. At the start of this season carrying the flag for the 125th anniversary of the club alongside the likes of Billy McNeill and Danny McGrain was humbling. As we walked around the pitch at the Celtic–Aberdeen curtain-raiser all I could hear was: 'There's only one Johnny Hartson.' It's such a rush to hear the fans singing your name like that. I have grown up now, I'm a dad of four, making my way as a coach and I have learned what a privileged position I am in.

Every time I come back to Paradise now the reception I get is awesome and it is something I truly appreciate. These are the sunshine times but in my darkest days I knew I could count on the Celtic family to help me pull through.

1

THE GAFFER

'John, you are immortal now.'

Liverpool boss Bill Shankly stood in the chaotic dressing room of the Estadio Nacional in Lisbon and uttered those unforgettable words to his great friend Jock Stein. He was right.

The man he called John had just won the 1967 European Cup for Celtic, masterminding a 2-1 final win over the legendary Helenio Herrera's Inter Milan. It was a victory for style and attacking flair over steel and defensive negativity. Jock's buccaneering Hoops overcame the *catenaccio* system Herrera had crafted.

In Italian, if you literally translate *catenaccio* it means 'door-bolt'. Well, big Jock found a way to kick the door in with those goals from Tommy Gemmell and Stevie Chalmers that are seared into the memory banks of every Celtic supporter now. For me, that was a triumph not just for the Celtic way but for the soul of football itself. That's why there can be only one gaffer for my Celtic Dream Team. Jock Stein. And unlike the rest of my Dream Team, for me, there's really no debate to be had on this one – it just has to be Jock Stein. Although having said that, there have, of course, been some other really great managers at Celtic Park over the years.

I think the fact that Jock won nine in a row and managed the team that became the first British side to win the European Cup means that there could be only one. The legend of Stein is something Billy McNeill has drummed into me every time I am lucky enough to have a chat with Cesar. I can count Billy as a friend through my time at the club and the work we often do together promoting our columns with the *Scottish Sun*. The big man would point to the bust of Jock, all the paintings, the fact that he has lounges and stands named after him at Celtic Park. He felt that was the least he deserved and I have always felt the history of Celtic is something those who follow the Lions should be proud of and try to live up to.

Martin O'Neill always told me that at Nottingham Forest he felt the shadow of Brian Clough loomed over some of the men who followed him into the manager's office. He'd heard of people asking for all the pictures of Clough's success to be taken down because they feared they were haunting the place. Martin just didn't buy into that notion, that coaches or players should be fed up of being reminded of the glory of the past. He wanted us to see those photographs of Jock Stein and to try to emulate what teams like Stein's had achieved. Martin didn't live in Jock's shadow, but I always felt that the fact he was at a club Stein had managed inspired him.

O'Neill won the Treble in his first season against a Rangers team that it has been proved now was shelling out money beyond their means to attract star names from all over Europe. That was an incredible achievement. I obviously never had the privilege of working with Mr Stein but I got to watch Martin at work and that was an education. He's an incredible operator. I look back now and think that Martin gave Celtic their pride back and there was such a feel-good factor about his appointment.

He attracted the likes of Chris Sutton, Henrik Larsson, Alan Thompson, Neil Lennon and myself. We were big-name, big-game players on Premiership wages, which proved that Martin had the clout to change the wage structure at Celtic. That was vital if the balance of power was to be shifted. He got men around him he trusted and his Irish roots appealed to the fans – they felt he was one of their own. And the most important thing? He won his first Old Firm game 6-2 and he started beating Rangers!

I will never forget one of my first mornings at training at Barrowfield when I was trying to get my bearings and learn about Celtic. Sutty turned to me and said, 'Listen, big man, as long as we are above them across the road everything will be alright for us here.'

Sounds simple that, but it was true. That was the onus that was on us as Celtic players and I have always bought into that. And throughout those heady O'Neill years it was hammered into us how important it was to go to Ibrox and win.

With Martin, you never knew where you were, he kept you on your toes. One day he would be asking how my kids were when we passed in the corridor, the next day he would blank me! When you were out of order you were generally told within the four walls of his office. Publicly, though, he would always praise you and back you to the hilt, and that was how he established the special bond he had with our team. Every one of us respected him and he got every shred he could out of players like Stan Varga, Ramon Vega, Momo Sylla and Steve Guppy. Those guys are good examples of players who were not big-cheque star names but who made a telling contribution because they reacted to his management. They wanted to do it for him and that's what O'Neill has, and that's what for me is the secret of his success: he gives you belief in yourself and you go out there every match day wanting to do well for him.

Even the master craftsmen like Henrik held him in such high esteem and he knew what made guys like them tick too. Every player needs to be managed in some way, whether it is an arm round the shoulder or a kick up the arse. The trick is to understand what they need to get the best out of themselves.

I hear people talk about who should replace Sir Alex Ferguson at Manchester United and I have to say I think of Martin O'Neill. He would NEVER have lived with a director of football or any of that nonsense, he'd have given scouts their place but no one would sign a player over his head.

On the coaching ground Steve Walford worked with us in the main and you wouldn't see Martin there as often as you would see a Strachan or a Redknapp. Martin would be back at the club but on a Friday or a Saturday, that's when he earned his money. He would tell you about the week before, where you had gone wrong or things you had done right.

I reflected when I talked to big Billy and Jinky Johnstone about Jock that there were a lot of similarities between him and Martin. Billy and Jinky wanted to win that European Cup for him, and Stein gave them a mission to believe in. And when you look back at our run to the UEFA Cup final, we really had no right to be going down south and beating the likes of Blackburn Rovers and Liverpool. We overcame Juventus, lived with Barcelona and that was because of O'Neill, in my eyes.

Some people said that Martin should have been on the training pitch more. I don't hold much truck with that argument because he knew everything that went on there, believe me. I used to think that he was hiding up a tree because by 12 o'clock when you came back to Celtic Park for lunch, he'd know if you'd had a howler in the morning. He was a master man-manager, he had faith in the team around him and he knew when to delegate.

There's one story about Martin that still makes me smile when I think back, although it didn't at the time, right enough. We were playing Dundee United in the Scottish Cup semi-final at Hampden and I had just set up the winner for Shaun Maloney. Now, I wasn't having the best of games but I had held up the ball magnificently to put the wee man in. There's about twenty minutes left and I sense that's the pivotal moment in the match. Then I look over to the touchline and the sub's board is up and it's got number 10 on it. He's bringing me off . . . again. And I'm raging.

Now there was nothing that Martin hated more than a player when he was being subbed walking off straight down the tunnel. I knew that. But the steam was coming out of my ears, so when Steve Walford came down from that Hampden technical area with the jacket to give me to join my team-mates I threw it back at him and stormed inside in a fury.

I got into the Hampden dressing room and launched a plate of sandwiches all over the place. There was tuna on Henrik Larsson's good suit, prawns in Neil Lennon's good black shoes. There was food all over the place. I was in a seethe and then all of the boys came bouncing in, we'd won the game, we were in the final.

Martin took one look around at the carnage and of my sandwich tantrum and he said, 'What the **** is the matter with you?' Now no one took on Martin O'Neill – it just wasn't a good idea. I only ever really saw myself, Thommo, Lenny and Henrik attempt it in our days there. None of us won.

I said to him, 'What the **** did you bring me off for?'

He just glared at me, ordered me to sit back down and said, 'Listen, John, in this game that we like to call football we sometimes have to run around a little bit. You, son, were not ****ing running around any more.'

O'Neill 1, Hartson 0. What do you say to that?

Movies like *Any Given Sunday* and TV shows like *Friday Night Lights* have built a kind of mystique around team talks and their value to top-level sportsmen. When Martin talked you listened and I'd say his most inspirational was on the night we beat Liverpool at Anfield on the way to Seville. They were the holders of the UEFA Cup that year and I just remember him speaking with such passion.

'This is what it's all about, no one beats Liverpool under the lights in Europe, but we CAN.'

He kept building it up about how no one fancied us, they were there for us to take, and that's exactly what we did. We roared out of the dressing room that night and I look upon that game as career defining. I scored the goal of my life; Martin had me in great shape. I was number 9 for Wales and number 10 for Celtic, I was lean and fit and hungry.

If you look at me celebrating my thirty-yarder that night, the ball that flew into the net with my parents standing behind the goal, and you see a guy in the prime of his life. The veins are popping out of my neck, I look like a machine. I was the footballer that Martin O'Neill had created. I will always show that goal to my kids and remember the level that Martin got me to. I'd just missed a penalty in the League Cup final defeat against Rangers and he lifted my chin off the floor so I could do what I did at Anfield.

People forget the stage I was at when Celtic came in for me. I was so fretful about my fitness that I refused to allow myself to get excited about the prospect of a move to Celtic. I had previously been turned down by Spurs, Charlton, Rangers and Coventry City on medicals and I felt the odds were slim I would pass one. Then Martin made the phone call that was to change my life.

He said, 'John, unless you have a hole in your heart then I will be signing you for Celtic. Get yourself on the plane to Glasgow. You are going to be my centre-forward.'

After all I had been through I wanted to run out to my back garden, punch the air and scream, 'I AM going to Celtic!'

So the debt I owe Martin O'Neill will never be repaid, really. He deserves to be mentioned in the same breath as Jock Stein but Martin would forgive me for my choice of manager. He knows the history.

My second manager at Celtic, Gordon Strachan, will never be every Hoops fan's cup of tea. People kept looking back at him as an Aberdeen player when he inspired such hatred that a Hoops fan ran on the pitch and attacked him. I never got that, I felt it was silly because this was Strachan, the coach and manager we were supposed to be judging, not Strachan the player. Judge him for his achievements and the record books will show you that he won three in a row for Celtic, which was something even Martin couldn't manage. Then he got the club to the last 16 of the Champions League and he deserves huge credit for that too.

I thought Gordon had a lot of imagination as a boss. I felt for instance that the signing of Shunsuke Nakamura was a masterstroke. Strachan was the hardest-working boss I ever played under. He lived for his job and he wanted to take the free-kicks and corners in training! He tried to improve players, that's what he lives for, and he would have the likes of Aiden McGeady and Shaun Maloney back for afternoon training because he saw something in them.

The media relationships were spikey with him and he didn't suffer fools gladly. My take on that was there may have been a lack of confidence there. A lot of press men thought he was a smart-arse, but I have to say I felt he was just a little nervous of having them in his world, of having them judge him.

Me? He helped me through some dark times in my life when my marriage was breaking up and it was shattering me as a footballer. I have the utmost respect for him as a man and as a coach, and when I was hanging by a thread and fighting the curse of my cancer, he called every day. You can't buy that sort of support, especially at a time when I wasn't his player any more, and my dad has never forgotten that either. I think that's when you learn who your friends are. I know who was round about my bed and calling when I was at death's door, and Gordon Strachan was one of those people. I have turned my life around now by recognising those who cared about me genuinely when I was at my lowest ebb and I know Gordon was on that list. So to those Celtic fans who don't give him a fair crack of the whip, this is all I will say: there is an insight to the man and you can judge for yourself if that changes your mind.

There was my illness and there was the death of Tommy Burns, and that's when you saw the real Gordon. It was Strachan who brought Tommy back into the first-team set-up as a coach and I got a year to work with TB that I will always treasure. Tommy's death left Gordon in tatters and when his face crumpled then I thought you saw the heart of a true football man who had lost a friend he cherished. That is Gordon for me; get past the other stuff. In time at Celtic I hope he is judged on his record and not the fact he got some fans' backs up.

Tommy Burns loomed large in my time at Celtic, he was a telling influence on myself and so many of the players brought into the club from the English Premiership. I was struck by his humility and his love for the Hoops, it was so infectious. We spoke a lot about the trials and tribulations, the good times and the bad he'd had at the place. He wouldn't have swapped it, any of it. Not even the dark days when he was a manager under fire and at war with Fergus McCann.

I think when you examine the history, it seems that Celtic players who become managers of the club tend to go through a world of hurt, and that just seems to be the hand that fate deals them. Tommy moulded a side together that played free-flowing, entertaining football.

They delivered the brand of this game that is associated with the club, the Glasgow Celtic Way. On the deck, fast movement out to the wingers with strikers that you could idolise. The sad thing for Tommy was that he was producing that sort of football against the greatest Rangers team of all time. That's the tag the boys who won nine in a row for Gers deserve to carry.

That must have been so hard for a Hoops diehard like Tommy to bear. I watched so many of those Old Firm games when I was down south and you would see Celtic dominate the game, be the better team. Then Alan McLaren or Richard Gough would make a death-defying clearance. Or more often than not, Andy Goram – now my fellow columnist at the *Scottish Sun* – would produce a save that beggared belief like that one from Pierre van Hooijdonk's overhead kick at Ibrox. It summed up Tommy's dignity and his respect for the ability of his rivals when he said, 'They will put that on my tombstone, "Andy Goram broke his heart".'

Yet I think it speaks volumes for Tommy that he was nowhere near the most successful manager of Celtic, yet fifteen years after he was sacked by Fergus McCann people still talk about his teams and the joy they got from watching them. They weren't winning trophies regularly, as Tommy only had the 1995 Scottish Cup final win over Airdrie to savour in three torrid years in charge. Yet there are great memories from the fans of a man who could talk to you all day about how he loved to nurture young footballers into better players and better people. I'd hear him telling them on the training field, 'Run with your head up, don't be looking down at the ball. Try and see the big picture.'

That was Tommy. He was all about educating players into how he felt the game should be played. I think he takes a lot of credit from his time as Celtic manager, although they were starved of silverware. Players like Andreas Thom, Pierre van Hooijdonk, Jorge Cadete and Paolo di Canio still live in the memory and they all idolised the manager who brought them to Scotland.

The song that tells you all about the Glasgow Celtic Way is precious to the fans and it's rightly part of the ethos of the club. Tommy lived by it but it didn't bring him the success he craved – I mean there was one season where he lost just one league game but still didn't win the title. That's ridiculously unlucky.

Me? I worked under the likes of Wenger, Redknapp, Kinnear, Hughes and Toshack but not one of them topped Martin O'Neill and he lived by the rules of what he always called 'The Winning Business'. He was by far the best manager I played under because for five years of my career he made me as a player. He once said to me, 'You know, John, the truth of what I do for a living is that a manager is only ever two games from the sack.' I walked away from that conversation thinking it would never happen to him at Celtic but I could see where his logic came from. He just realises that it's a precarious occupation. Lose two games against the bottom three and people start asking questions.

That's why he called it 'The Winning Business'. He knew our midfield could malfunction, our strikers could have an off day but if someone sclaffed one in through the keeper's legs with five minutes to go then the bulk of the fans would go home relatively happy. Draw that same game and we could go off to a hail of boos. That's the fine margins you live with as a manager of a club like Celtic.

In the O'Neill era we didn't always play great football but we had a genius in Henrik Larsson who could score out of nothing. Stan Petrov might roam in from midfield and nick one, Steve Guppy could stick it on someone's head or Alan Thompson had the ability to produce a bit of magic. More often than not, we would get away with it. Yet the skill level that we possessed in that Seville side was for me far too often underestimated. Lambert and Lennon were overlooked, yet they were very accomplished midfielders in their differing ways. And in Hartson, Sutton and Larsson Celtic had three strikers who at that time could have played for ANY Premier League side in England. I'd stand by that statement any day of the week.

I understand fans clinging to the Glasgow Celtic Way and I applaud it but in the modern era football is all about winning and, believe me, Tommy was no dreaming purist, he understood that. He also knew that he got longer than some may have got in that hot-seat because of the football he was producing and the fact that he is one of Celtic's own.

Neil Lennon carries that same aura with him, yet I don't think for some reason that Tony Mowbray ever did. Neil is seen as one of the Celtic family and he was given breathing space after the European exits against Utrecht, Braga and Sion because of that. Mowbray never had that luxury, he was bulleted after a run of bad results just as Kenny Dalglish was at Liverpool last season. Yet I understand why Tony took the job. He had captained the club, he even invented The Huddle and the club meant such a lot to him. I'm sure after what happened to him at Celtic, Mogga walked away feeling he had a black mark on his reputation as a manager. His pride will have hurt – just as Lou Macari's did sixteen years earlier – because he knows that for some reason he failed on a stage he desperately wanted to succeed on.

Celtic and Rangers are more different beasts than you will find almost anywhere else on Planet Football. Look at Paul Le Guen at Rangers, who arrived with such a massive reputation from France. Sir David Murray looked like the cat who got the cream on the day he was appointed and said he would be a moonbeam of success. Yet within 200 days Le Guen had dropped skipper Barry Ferguson, stripped him of the captaincy, there was civil war at Ibrox and PLG was gone.

I hope that in the passage of time the Celtic fans will come to look at the reigns of the likes of Macari and Mowbray and realise that it simply didn't work for them, it was not for lack of effort or commitment or knowledge. It just didn't click. It shouldn't sully their legacy as Celtic players. I will be able to take my 110 goals for the club to my grave, and it should be the same for Lou and Tony, who wore the strip with pride and excelled, in my eyes. When they return to the club they should not be given a hard time, I think the Celtic fans can be bigger than that.

I have a lot of respect for Mowbray. He was my manager at my final club, West Bromwich Albion, and he was someone you could trust. He is from a solid working-class background in Middlesbrough and he is a man's man. I almost couldn't bear to watch that final 4-0 defeat at St Mirren that spelled the end for him. It is hard to watch a man you like being almost broken by a job he wanted so much.

Remember Celtic paid £2 million in compensation for Tony and he was seen as the dream ticket appointment who would give the fans the type of football they wanted. Yet the pressure told, the endless hunger for victories killed him. It's like Brendan Rodgers at Liverpool now. If he loses four games in a row then questions are going to be asked about his future. Do that at Swansea and no one would have batted an eyelid.

You know, a couple of years ago I applied for the Swansea City job, but with hindsight now I wouldn't have done that. I'm a local lad there and the pressure of managing my heroes would have been too much because I have to live in the city too. Look at Lenny right now when he puts on such a calm exterior and endures a lot of stick. Neil is my friend but I still don't truly know how he feels inside about all the horrible abuse he has taken.

He has had to cope with death threats and that hurt me to see Glasgow, a city I love, portrayed to the world at large as this dark place full of hate. Glasgow is not like that, you have to tread carefully sometimes and be a role model to the kids who have your poster on their bedroom walls. Still, though, it can also be a wonderful place full of warmth and humour.

All I can say, though, about a football manager getting bombs and bullets in the post is try and take yourself out of the cauldron for a minute and think like a foreigner. If you read that stuff would you want to come and work here? Didn't think so. If people are going to stoop that low and threaten your family, we have got to a stage where this is nothing to do with football. I mean Neil had police escorts, he lived in a safehouse for a spell, he had 24-hour guards on his house. I don't care how big or strong or tough you are, nobody should have to live their life like that. You should be able to walk down the street without people screaming abuse at you. It shocked the world of football outside of Scotland and it didn't show the country I have taken to my heart in a good light.

I felt for Neil because I totally disagree with this notion that he brings it on himself. Look, in England Sir Alex Ferguson is the prime wind-up merchant who plays mind-games with opponents all the time. Fergie doesn't get death threats, neither does Walter Smith, so why does Neil Lennon get them? He's just a football manager working to get better at what he does.

Neil is now trying to live up to a legacy that was created by Willie Maley, Celtic's first ever manager. It'd be a great quiz question to ask your pals who the youngest ever Hoops boss was, because it was Maley. He was given the nod as secretary-manager at the age of just twenty-nine. He won the title in his first full season and in forty-three years as the boss he won sixteen league titles, fourteen Scottish Cups, fourteen Glasgow Cups and nineteen Glasgow Charity Cups. No wonder he's got his own song! Throughout his reign, Maley – who never had team talks and watched games from the directors' box – showed he was a master at constructing teams. He was the man who signed Jimmy McGrory, who scored 550 top-class goals and 408 in 408 league matches. Unreal stat, that. McGrory succeeded Maley as Celtic manager and had almost twenty years in the hot-seat without threatening the same sort of success as his mentor. He did, however, mastermind a 7-1 triumph over Rangers in the 1957 League Cup final. I know the song now, 'Oh Hampden in the Sun . . . Celtic 7 the Rangers 1'. Wouldn't have minded playing that day!

Wille Maley, Jimmy McGrory, Jock Stein . . . all these great names have contributed to a remarkable football story and it was always one that I wanted to learn. I read up the books, I went on the internet and I wanted to learn the history. That's not something that ever consumed me at West Ham United or Wimbledon.

As a Welshman, I am proud of big Jock's links to my country, a part of his life that a lot of people forget. He played at and managed Llanelli and there is still a Jock Stein Lounge at the club there. So many people don't realise just how much they should treasure that link, and every time I am at the club I try to educate people about the legend that is Stein. I tell them what he stood for and point out that Sir Alex Ferguson idolised Jock, which shows the pedigree of the man. Fergie learned so much from Jock in their days together with Scotland and I always feel the way he talks about him, the reverence he shows, is telling. I was fortunate in my time at Celtic that I was able to have many chats with the likes of Billy McNeill and Jimmy Johnstone. They just regarded Jock Stein as a genius and what he brought to the Hoops was phenomenal. The day I walked into Celtic I realised this was a different club from all the others I had played for.

Now when people ask me what it is that make the Hoops special, I tell them two things: the fans and the history. I could have said the Johnstones and the Larssons, mentioned all the great players but ultimately no one man is bigger than Celtic. That's what I have learned. The club will always be there and for me; it's not about the stars and the icons that the place creates. It's simply about those two things, the fans and the history. It's just an unbelievable place and the fact is that Jock Stein and his Lisbon Lions put Celtic on the map. Leeds United, Manchester United and all the English superpowers dreamed of it but it was Jock and those Lisbon Lions who put Celtic firmly on the football map. They planted the flag for us. That team made Celtic a worldwide club and, in my opinion, every player should learn the story of the club.

I made a vow to myself the day I walked into the place that I wanted to write my own chapter. Deep down I knew that I would never be perceived in the same way as, say, Henrik Larsson. I wasn't that type of player, I even knew I couldn't hit the heights of Chris Sutton, who I regarded as another very special player, so I came to terms with that and I sat and thought about whether there was a way I could secure my place in the folklore. And the answer was easy: go out and score 100 goals for Celtic. I knew there were only twenty-odd players in the history of the club who had done that and I felt I had it in my power to be one of them. So I set myself a target and I got there by scoring 110 goals that mean the world to me. I also felt big Jock would have approved. He made me want to be a part of the history and I think that's what his presence around the place still does for new signings the minute they walk in the door.

So for my Celtic Dream Team I have this image of a manager's door ready to welcome all these great players. And the plaque on that door has to say Mr Stein.

2

FROM THE HOLY GRAIL TO THE HOLY GOALIE

I stood in an Edinburgh church the day the Celtic family said goodbye to Ronnie Simpson and felt humbled and privileged. I was an injured Hoops star representing the club at the funeral back in April 2004 after a heart attack took the Lisbon Lions' goalkeeper from us at the age of seventy-three. Amidst the grief that day I remember the pride of Ronnie's family in his achievements and the smile on his former skipper Billy McNeill's face as he recalled the veteran keeper the Lions simply called 'Faither'. Big Billy paid a glowing tribute to Ronnie, and I can still feel the raw emotion of his speech that day. They had such a special bond between them, that team. They were all born within thirty miles of Celtic Park yet they went on to become the first British side to grasp football's Holy Grail and win the European Cup.

The year 2012 saw the 45th anniversary of that triumph in Lisbon and I know people nowadays sometimes tire of the recounting of the tales of that glory day. Me? I can't get enough of it. I could have picked this Dream Team and gone for the entire Lisbon Lions side in some ways but that would been betraying so many other greats who wore the Hoops. Still there can be no question that the first serious contender for the goalkeeper's jersey in this Heaven's Eleven has to be Ronnie Simpson and I will always remember that funeral and how Billy spoke of Ronnie's ability and his bravery.

I've watched the fantastic footage of that 2-1 European Cup final win over Inter Milan and other films of games of the Lions in a bid for the evidence I'd need to assess Ronnie as a keeper. The Lions were built on the bedrock of Simpson's reliability and from what Billy told me I think it is fair to say that Ronnie was unorthodox – he'd stop shots with his elbows and his shoulders if he had to. And what all his team-mates respected him for the most was that he'd done something few footballers ever managed: he made Jock Stein change his mind.

Big Jock was the manager at Hibs when Ronnie was there and there's no kind way to put this, he thought he was a slack-arse in training. Stein didn't fancy Simpson's laid-back attitude and offloaded him to Celtic for £4,000. God knows what Ronnie was thinking when Jock was appointed Celtic boss later that season! Sure enough, he was cover for John Fallon at first, but when Fallon was blamed for a Cup final defeat by Rangers, Simpson had the jersey. And until a dislocated shoulder ended his career at the age of forty, he never let it go.

Ronnie Simpson's story is a remarkable one. Top-team debut at the age of just fourteen for Queen's Park in 1945, he was the youngest player ever to represent a Scottish League club. Matt Busby picked him for the 1948 Great Britain Olympic squad and he lost a bronze medal play-off with Denmark. And with two FA Cup winner's medals with Newcastle United under his belt and that spell at Hibs before signing for Celtic at the age of thirty-four, they said he was in the twilight of his career and was winding down. Ronnie knew different.

When I studied his career before we sat down to write this book, I think that's what impressed me most about Ronnie. Mental strength. At 5'10" he wasn't blessed with the best physical attributes for a goalkeeper, he even used to stand on his tiptoes in the team photographs to look taller! Yet still he harnessed his skills and made the most of them to become a European Cup winner. More than that, he convinced one of the greatest managers who ever lived to think again and put his trust in him.

I was gone from this game with my desire drained and my body feeling broken before my thirty-third birthday, so that's why I have always admired those who make the sacrifices to keep going as the big Four-Zero looms, just as Ronnie did. I played with some superb goalkeepers in my time but when I sat down in my study with a blank piece of paper to begin this project, Ronnie Simpson's name had to be one of the first I wrote down for consideration on the list of Celtic's greatest goalkeepers. He carved it in the folklore of the club winning nine in a row, he was a Lisbon Lion and I've been lucky enough to sit in the company of Billy McNeill and John Clark and hear them tell his story.

They loved the tale of his debut for Queen's Park in the Summer Cup at fourteen and the fact that his life in the game went full circle. Ronnie, whose old man Jimmy had fourteen caps for his country, was also the OLDEST player to make his Scotland debut at the age of thirty-six. The game? England at Wembley in 1967, when Scotland beat the World Cup holders 3-2 to become the unofficial champions of the world. I've had some good seasons in my life but a domestic Treble, the European Cup and a win over England in one campaign? That's a life less ordinary, and Ronnie Simpson lived it.

The day I joined Celtic in 2001 I realised this was more than a football club. Martin O'Neill sanctioned a £6 million fee for me, a fair chunk of the £20 million-plus I cost clubs over my career. Yet here I sensed this was a place where the pounds and the pence didn't count so much, this was about the passion and the pride. The history. A huge part of that story is John Thomson, the Prince of Goalkeepers, who died on September 5, 1931 at the age of just twenty-two following an accidental collision with Rangers striker Sam English in an Old Firm match. I have read his tragic story and tried to take in the enormity of it all, the sense of loss. After my own brush with death when I was diagnosed with testicular cancer and it spread to my brain, I feel I do have a perspective on what his family must have gone through.

I never had the honour of seeing John play, you can only rely on the words written about him but it's staggering to think that at the age of twenty-two he already had 211 games for the Hoops under his belt. One thing I know for sure: his legend will always live on.

The nature of this book takes us deep into the history of Celtic at times and a lot of the interest has been in finding out about some players we knew little about, those whose stories are sometimes lost in the mists of time. Guys like Charlie Shaw.

There's this brilliant website called The Celtic Wiki where you can discover the tales of heroes you may not have heard of, and we had to go there researching the keepers. Shaw, it emerges, was just 5'6" but was revered between the sticks for the Hoops. He joined Celtic from Queen's Park Rangers in May 1913 for £250, and it was money well spent. Charlie won his way into the fans' hearts with his athleticism belying his lack of inches. In 1913-14 he lost only fourteen goals in thirty-eight games with twenty-six shut-outs. A Celtic record that still stands.

Shaw was made Celtic skipper, a job rarely handed to keepers in those days, and fought the Parkhead board-room over the low wages the players were paid. He never betrayed his roots or the working-class values he had been given in the mining village of Twechar. As a Welsh-man, I relate to that. When he was released in 1925, Charlie Shaw walked out of the exit door with 436 games for Celtic to his name and 240 clean sheets. He had won six league titles and two Scottish Cups. That compares favourably to any of my contenders and that's why he made the list.

Charlie's adventurous spirit meant that he moved across the Atlantic to the USA where he starred for New Bedford Whalers FC, the leading football side in the States at that time, as their player-manager. He died of pneumonia in New York in 1938, having carved his name in Celtic's folklore.

No list of great Celtic keepers would be complete without Packie Bonner. He is a Celtic hero and I under-stand the status that he has with the fans – he has earned a place in their hearts. He played 642 games for Celtic and he had a terrific consistency, but perhaps all the big memories of him are with the Republic of Ireland rather than his club days. Packie had twenty years at the club and was a terrific keeper. Think of the name Bonner and your mind always drags you back to Italia 90 and THAT penalty save from Romania's Daniel Timofte that helped take Jack Charlton's Irish to the last eight of the World Cup Italy. Toto Schillaci would gobble up a rebound after Packie parried Roberto Donadoni's pile-driver but his place in a nation's psyche was secure.

Bonner won four titles at Celtic – three Scottish Cups and a League Cup – but suffered perhaps from having to live through Rangers winning their nine in a row. In truth and if we are totally honest here, goalkeeper has often been a problem position for Celtic. Across the city, Rangers' greatest ever goalkeeper, Andy Goram, left and was replaced by the brilliant German Stefan Klos, who quit and the excellent Allan McGregor, now of Turkish side Besiktas and who I rate very highly, then took over. Even in the midst of all the chaos there has been at Ibrox, when McGregor refused to transfer his contract to the newco and accept life in Division Three after his club lurched into liquidation, the replacement is Neil Alexander, who again is a decent shot-stopper. They've been able to rely on those sort of keepers, but often Celtic have not.

Artur Boruc had it in him to change all that but, in my opinion, he messed up his Celtic career. That sounds stark, brutal and perhaps a little harsh, but for me it's the truth. The supporters loved him but I will always feel that Artur could have been a true legend of the club. He could have gone on to be so much more for Celtic. He had great spring, he had all the attributes and there were days when I faced him in training and he was almost unbeatable. Boruc was also a modern-day goalkeeper in that he could handle the pass-back rule easily and was very comfortable with the ball at his feet. Artur, when he was focused, worked so hard in training but then I firmly believe that all the adulation and the hero worship of him as 'The Holy Goalie' went to his head.

He got involved with some aspects of being a Celtic player – like waving Champions' flags at Ibrox – that appeals to a certain element of the crowd but not all of them. So in the eyes of many I know, he would be the fans' choice for Dream Team keeper and that's why he is on the list despite what I would assess as a Hoops career that was not properly fulfilled.

The season I had playing with Artur under Gordon Strachan marked us out as kindred spirits in some ways. He often looked like he enjoyed a drink and the odd long lunch off the pitch! We both fought with our weight but, like me, when he played well, no one mentioned it.

As ever in football it's only when you slip up and make a mistake that it gets dragged up, and Artur was playing in the cruellest positions of all for that. I know what being a Celtic idol means. I have been lucky enough to have that song belted out when I scored my goals:

> There's only one Johnny Hartson,
> There's only one Johnny Hartson.
> He's got no hair, but we don't care,
> Walking in a Hartson wonderland.

Still gives me goosebumps, that one. So I know how Artur felt when those wonderful fans took him into their hearts and dubbed him 'The Holy Goalie'. Boruc was massive for Gordon Strachan in his first year at the club and he will always be remembered with such fondness.

You need big balls to play for Celtic and Rangers, I always tell that to anyone I talk to in England about my experiences. You've got to have steel inside you, be a character. Boruc had that but he made gestures towards the Rangers fans at times that were not the wisest and angered the media.

The Celtic fans ate it up, though, and the legend of the Holy Goalie kept growing. There is a line, though, isn't there? Are you having fun with the hype or are you starting to believe it? I feel now that is what happened with Artur Boruc. He believed the hype and it cost him the chance to be a true Celtic legend. Too often towards the end he was on the front pages instead of the back and I know from my own experiences with my own divorce that when you are at a low ebb in your personal life then Glasgow is the sort of city that can eat you up.

Artur split from his wife and found a new partner during his Celtic days and I suffered through that myself. The scrutiny on you as an Old Firm player on and off the pitch is intense and in all honesty I couldn't get out of the city quick enough back then. So I have sympathy for Boruc because of that and I think the pressure on him in Glasgow would have been a huge factor in him deciding to move to Italy and Fiorentina.

In some ways he had taken liberties with this great football city and what it can offer you and I think when Artur looks back he might acknowledge that. I was just like him and I got dragged into it all at one time, and I wish now I had done some things differently in my five years at Celtic. I chose some of the friends in my circle badly, I went through a very painful divorce in the public eye in a divided city and that's why I think I am qualified to look at the Boruc situation and assess it through the eyes of someone who has been there.

Glasgow now is a place I relish returning to – great bars and restaurants and warm people who respect me for the 110 goals I scored for Celtic in my time there. Yet I also know the pitfalls of the place as a player, you can be hailed by some and hated by others. There are Rangers fans who meet me now who are staggered when we have a chat. They shake their heads and say, 'I have to tell you the truth big man, I used to HATE you.' That was simply down to the colours I wore. Nothing to do with my roots on a Swansea council estate or how I have lived my life.

I just feel that's how it was with Artur. With both of us the critics will always say that if we'd been two stones lighter we'd have been superstars. I have been told my natural ability should have taken me to Real Madrid but I can still look back now and feel that I had a career many players would love to swap for. Still, deep down, I also know I could have tuned in a bit better as regards to extra training, been a little more disciplined with my diet, and who knows then? I think that's the Boruc Syndrome! Yes, he was a huge favourite with the Hoops fans but for me he could have been world-class and a superstar on the world stage. It's always disappointing when you see someone with the limitless potential Artur had and he doesn't quite manage to fulfil it. He will have watched those Poland games in his home nation at Euro 2012 with a heavy heart. He must have. Yet in any list of Celtic number 1s the man they called the Holy Goalie simply has to be on it.

In my own team, Rab Douglas took the rap for our defeat in the UEFA Cup final and I have heard a lot of people saying we would have beaten Porto with someone like Boruc between the sticks. The big fella has always been called the weak link of that terrific side that Martin O'Neill put together and I always felt that was bang out of order. Rab worked his bollocks off in training and he never thought he was the best keeper in the world. Instead he recognised his deficiencies and he worked on them so hard to improve as a keeper. Rab and I would have competitions on the scales because we both needed to do extra sessions with our fitness coach, Jim Hendry, to try and keep our weight down.

Look back at his career, he took the number 1 jersey from Jonathan Gould and he withstood the challenge of Magnus Hedman for his jersey. Javier Sánchez Broto never got the right contract sorted out at the club and Rab just hung in there and kept a job that I know he treasured. I know that the gaffer looked to replace him a couple of times but whenever a challenge presented itself, Rab saw them off. So, the weak link? Never in my eyes – they just say that because they look throughout that team and see so many true Celtic greats.

The UEFA Cup final was so tight on the night in Seville that when you come so close to history and lose 3-2 in extra-time then I think the fans in their sense of desolation at being so near and yet so far begin the search for scapegoats. I have always felt that Rab got an unlucky break on Derlei's heartbreaking extra-time clincher on that broiling night, and I will always feel that he got a raw deal in the aftermath. He became an easy target to pin the blame on but there was not one finger inside our dressing room pointing at Rab Douglas.

I felt very comfortable when I looked back and saw Rab in the goal for us, for every isolated howler people pick out now there are outstanding performances like the one he had in the Mestalla against Valencia. We would have lost that game 5-0 without the big man that night. He was immense. He also had a sore one when a Gregory Vignal shot careered off him and went in to give Rangers an Old Firm win. If ever there is a game you don't want to make a blunder in it's that one! I scored a host of penalties for Celtic in huge situations but the only one anyone ever wants to talk about is the one I missed in the last minute when we lost 2-1 in the League Cup final at Hampden. So I reckon I am qualified to talk about how Rab feels about that.

I think when you examine the history of Celtic keepers it is fair to call it our problem position. There have been those who threatened to make a real mark, like Gordon Marshall, who cost £270,000 when he came to the club from Falkirk back in 1991. Big Marsh was an able keeper and would go on to make exactly 100 league appearances in seven years at the club. He landed a Scotland cap against the USA but again never quite sparkled in the job and left for Killie in 1998. Truth is, for an outfield player, whilst you may sympathise with your goalkeeper when he makes an error and rally behind him, you will never truly understand him. Those boys are an alien breed. I watch them training and think they're just so different from proper footballers!

Seriously, that was one of the things that was different with the best keeper I ever played with. Neville Southall could hold his own in the five-a-side games with us when I was on international duty with Wales. He had amazing feet for such a big fella and was just a blinding keeper. We've had Peter Shilton, David Seaman, Gordon Banks and Pat Jennings and the like, but I still think big Nev is the best British keeper of all time. Big Nev has a record ninety-two caps for Wales and was a true legend with Everton. Southall, like Ronnie Simpson, was often classed as an unorthodox keeper but I know he lived by the rule that it didn't matter how you stopped them – as long as you stopped them.

Neville worked at all sorts of jobs before he was a full-time footballer. He was a binman, a waiter and a hod carrier and I always felt that was what made him such a down-to-earth fella. He just loved his football and he racked up some amazing stats, as he simply refused to hang up his gloves. He was forty-one when he played in the Premiership for Bradford City in 2000 and they lost 2-1 to Leeds United. Their goals came from Michael Bridges who was twenty years younger than Nev! Southall finally chucked it when he was forty-four years old at Dagenham and Redbridge. He'd played 979 top-class games.

How good was he? Well, *World Soccer* named him one of the top 100 players of the twentieth century. He was that good. I played and trained with him, and they were right. Southall had agility and reflexes to die for and one-on-one he was an intimidating presence – even in training. If you nicked one past him you knew you had earned it and you were on your game.

When I was at Arsenal, Seaman was top man and I always thought he was one of those players who suffered because people would always pick on the negatives when they assessed him. Rather than look at the brilliance and the saves he produced week in and week out for the Gunners, they would focus on the goal he lost to Ronal-dinho for England in the 2002 World Cup against Brazil when that free-kick looped in over his head. Or they would hark back to that 1995 European Cup Winners' Cup final when Nayim launched one from the halfway line and it sailed in. Two goals through an entire career – it's an injustice to make that your memory of a guy I felt was top drawer, and I should know, because I faced him in training every day.

The best I played against? Well, that would surprise you because I would plump for Tim Flowers of Blackburn Rovers. The year Rovers won the Premiership I remember big Tim making a string of saves from myself and Ian Wright one night at Ewood Park that were beyond belief. He was like a cat; he would just pull them out of the air. When they won that title under Kenny Dalglish, everyone talked about the SAS partnership. Shearer and Sutton. Yes, they were key but for me the contribution of Flowers is always wrongly overlooked. I've faced the likes of Gianluigi Buffon with Italy, Stefan Klos at Rangers, but Flowers stands out for me.

It's always interesting to assess the present players against those of the past and see how they stack up. The current Hoops keeper, Fraser Forster, is big all right at 6'7" – compare that to Ronnie Simpson – and has the tools in his locker to go on and make himself a huge part of the club in the years to come. Last summer there was all sorts of speculation about Neil Lennon moving for this keeper or that one, but Forster had shown in his loan spells that he had the mentality to cope with the pressures of being the Celtic number 1. I know the goalkeeping coach, Stevie Woods, has had a massive influence on the big fella and it will be interesting to see how he develops now.

It did surprise me more than a little that Fraser didn't get looked at by the new England manager Roy Hodgson for the Euro 2012 squad with England, but I think you have to look at that now and tell the truth. Sure, Manchester City's Joe Hart is a lock-in for the top job, but behind him? Come on, be honest, England coaches DO ignore players when they are plying their trade in the SPL. How else do you explain Hodgson taking nineteen-year-old Birmingham City rookie Jack Butland to Euro 2012 ahead of Forster, who has been developing as a keeper in the white-hot atmosphere of Old Firm derbies? It doesn't make any sense.

Think about it, Celtic striker Gary Hooper was overlooked too because his goals were 'only' scored in Scotland. Well, scoring goals in the SPL didn't stop me having a great career for Wales, or Henrik Larsson becoming a legend with Sweden, did it? I'm not having that one, the English are putting themselves on a pedestal. Look at it. Chris Sutton and Alan Thompson were magnificent for Celtic during the Martin O'Neill years. Their sole honour was forty-five minutes for Thommo in one international, so I'm afraid Fraser Forster is going to have to live with that situation nagging away at him.

Chris Woods, Terry Butcher and Paul Gascoigne and the likes of them had proven themselves with England BEFORE they came to Rangers. Forster is trying to make his way in the game and will be desperate to break into the international set-up. Whether he can do it with the undoubted bias there is against Celtic and Rangers players down south now is another question.

Gary Hooper would score goals for any team in the world in any league in the world. If he was playing for

Manchester United he would score as many goals as Wayne Rooney. He is not in the same league as an all-round player but he is a natural goalscorer, and yet he too was overlooked for Euro 2012 for the likes of Manchester United kid, Danny Welbeck.

So in the future that is a big consideration for Forster: if he left Celtic he'd have a better chance of getting an England cap. I'm sorry but that's not just a viewpoint any more, that's a proven FACT. Who knows, though? Five years from now some other star of the past might embark on a project like this and the choice of keeper will be Fraser Forster of Celtic and England. I am not holding my breath, though. He is battling against a form of footballing prejudice.

In the end this debate on who should fill the number 1 jersey has been one that has intrigued me because I could delve into the history books to discover more about John Thompson and to find out for the first time about a character like Charlie Shaw, who must have been something else. His story alone deserves the Hollywood treatment from battling the disadvantages of being a 5'6" goalie to his fight for fair pay for his team-mates against the Parkhead boardroom and his journey to the States as a player-manager. Unbelievable.

In the end it comes down to three names for me: Simpson, Bonner and Boruc. I have watched as much footage as I could of Ronnie Simpson, I've studied Packie in depth and I played with the Holy Goalie. On this one I feel there is a wholly convincing case for the player I have chosen because he was between the sticks for Celtic on the greatest day in Scottish footballing history.

Ronnie Simpson overcame the initial scepticism of Jock Stein, he made the big man believe in him and for me has to get the nod. Besides, if I had gone for anyone else, I think Cesar would have killed me!

Yes, I think if you put yourself in my shoes here you have to trust the judgement of the captain of the Lisbon Lions who told me he would have trusted the man behind him with his life. That's good enough for me. That's the key reason why Ronnie Simpson is my Celtic Dream Team keeper.

3

THE RIGHT MAN FOR
THE RIGHT JOB

He was the best £50,000 Martin O'Neill ever spent – and the genius in the signing of Didier Agathe was that he was bought with a role already tailor-made for him. He'd come to Scotland from French football and sparkled on the right wing or up front at Raith Rovers, where his pace was always a real weapon. Then he won his way to Hibs and again they saw him as a striker, someone they could look to get balls in over the top of the defence to use his blistering acceleration. Then 'The Gaffer' came into his life and, in my eyes, the capture of Agathe was a masterstroke because he became probably the best Celtic have had in the last few decades in terms of a player who could give you that attacking menace down the right-hand side. He had an unbelievable engine and it is scary to think that Martin got him out of Hibs for such a paltry fee. He must go down as one of the best pieces of transfer business in the O'Neill era.

Didier wasn't a traditional right-back, of course, because Martin as a manager always loved and trusted the

3-5-2 system, and he still does. So Agathe was wide of our three towering centre-halves and he was such a superb outlet for us. Didier's main weakness, for me, was that he was just too nice. I don't mean that I wanted him to snap people in half and break their legs, it was just that sometimes you wanted him to grit his teeth and win a tackle and he wouldn't do that because he just didn't have an ounce of nastiness in his body. Maybe it was his laid-back upbringing on the island of La Reunion? He couldn't take the ball and the man in a challenge because that just wasn't in his nature, yet full-backs play in a position where you often have *carte blanche* to boot players up in the air and get away with it. Still, no matter how much I urged Didier to give someone the message in a game, he just couldn't bring himself to do it. He'd just smile then set off on another of those Roadrunner gallops up the wing! It must be the devil inside me but that was a source of major frustration to me and he looked at this mad Welshman telling him to stick the boot in with bemusement.

You know, in the olden days when you could dodge punishment from referees with the first tackle, I used to close my eyes in fear every time the winger got the ball first time against Stuart Pearce. They didn't call him 'Psycho' for nothing. Every game I played in, WALLOP! First time the winger got it they'd get cemented. Nowadays that sort of tackle will put you in the stand – instant red card. I used to always be pleading with the ref that it was my first tackle so I could leave my mark on a centre-half. At the start of my career you would get away with that sort of stuff. Second one in the book, third one he might think about a red. For a combative, aggressive player like myself those were the rules that you lived by. Now, though, you could see yourself red-carded within twenty seconds of the first whistle if you mis-time a tackle. That's how the game has changed, not for the better, in my opinion.

Didier, though, for all that he didn't possess that nasty streak, had pace like you wouldn't believe. He was the fastest at the club by a mile. He would beat a player three times in one run, and the fans loved it. They loved his buccaneering style when he was on form. Henrik and I hated it! By the time Didier got around to crossing the ball we'd have made three different runs and we'd be shouting, 'Just put the ****ing thing in.'

He was a natural athlete, though, a guy who floated around the pitch and he could have been even better with a killer final cross. He was frustrating, yes, but I still loved him as a player and he merits his mention in the candidates for a slot at right-back in my Dream Team.

Didier was a devout Catholic and I think the sweetness in the fella's soul was summed up by the fact that he would often go to the cemetery near our training ground and help an old widower repair the statue that was at his wife's grave. That was the measure of Agathe the man and he was never one for flashy watches or sports cars. He always told us he would go home and start a football academy and he has been as good as his word, trying to pave a way for other youngsters from La Reunion to make a name for themselves in the game. He's still playing too for a team called Jeunesse Sportive Saint-Pierroise on his home island.

Didier was a key player in helping us get to Seville but a measure of just how much he developed under Martin came in the European games with Barcelona the following season. Ronaldinho was at the peak of his powers then but he just couldn't shake Agathe off and he ended up applauding Didier at the end of those matches when he was so used to life the other way around. Agathe won three titles, three Scottish Cups and a League Cup, in his time at Celtic and although a spell under Martin at Aston Villa didn't work out, I think Didier's story is proof positive of the influence one manager can have on a player's life.

Jim Craig, like every Lisbon Lion, came into consideration here and I realise just what a solid and reliable presence he was in that special team. I've got to admit, I can never work out Jim's nickname 'Cairney'. Apparently it comes from an old TV show called *That Man Craig*. The actor who played the lead role was called John Cairney so Jim became Cairney!

That team had Faither in goals, Cairney at right-back, 'The Brush' and Cesar in the middle, they had 'Ten-Thirty', Jinky and 'Lemon' too. They liked their nicknames, the Lisbon Lions. Anyhow, I feel Cairney, if we can call him that, had to be right in the mix here.

I know from experience that footballers can be suspicious of a bit of intelligence in the dressing room. Jim was a dentistry student and a Glasgow Uni boy but he held his own in the banter, I'm told, and survived.

Craig was actually a Jimmy McGrory signing but fate brought him to the club just as Jock Stein was preparing to take over the hot-seat and – like O'Neill with Agathe – the master manager quickly noticed he had the role that fitted the player perfectly. Craig soon displaced Willie O'Neill and Ian Young and a Lion was being bred.

Yet when you look back at the footage of the final, Jim could so easily have been the scapegoat, as it was his tackle after seven minutes that gave Internazionale the penalty that Sandro Mazzola stuck away to give them the lead. Jim's recollections of Stein's reaction to that incident tell you so much about the psyche of a managerial genius. With Celtic 1-0 down at the break, the big man knew Craig had to go out and try to rescue the match. He didn't slaughter him, he threw an arm around his right-back and said, 'Don't worry, Cairney, that was never a penalty, never in a million years. Put it behind you, show them what you can do in the second half.'

The rest is history, as Craig tore forward up the right flank to tee up the measured pass for his opposite full-back, Tommy Gemmell, to rifle in that unforgettable equaliser. Yet at the end of the game Stein's face momentarily clouded over as he stared daggers at Craig amidst the celebrations and said, 'What on earth were you thinking about at the penalty? What a stupid tackle, you almost cost us the European Cup.'

That could be construed as meanness of spirit in some quarters but instead I choose to see that as the attention to detail of one of the greatest managers who ever walked the earth. Even in the moment of his greatest triumph Stein could still calm himself enough to look at the game with clarity and feel deep down that it WAS a penalty and that Craig had to learn from his mistake.

When I sit in Celtic company and talk of those Lions these days, some older fans will tell me that Jim was the weak link of that team, yet he won a Scotland cap and always had the foresight to be planning ahead for his future away from the game as a dentist. From the tales of the tunnel in Lisbon when all those swarthy Italians with the film-star looks were looking at our gang of toothless wonders, maybe he should have started practising on his own team-mates!

Jim had to come into my thinking for this side – every hero of Lisbon did – but when you look back at his career at Celtic you can see the factors towards the end of his Hoops days that meant he left the club at the age of just twenty-nine. Davie Hay, who would become such a combative midfielder and is in contention for a starting jersey elsewhere in this book, could operate at right-back and a young Danny McGrain was also emerging as a star of the future. Craig began to fade out of the picture. He didn't figure in the 1970 European Cup final defeat by Feyenoord but two years later, in the semi-final against Inter Milan, he had the bottle and bravery to take a shoot-out penalty and score. Sadly, Celtic still lost out in the lottery from the spot after two 0-0 draws, although the Italians would also taste defeat in the final against Ajax.

A major figure in one European Cup final, overlooked for another, scored a semi-final penalty two years later. Stop for a moment and think of the glory days Jim Craig lived through as a Celtic player. If the club had even a hint of that sort of success today, the newspapers would be felling forests to tell the story. It's fitting that such a decent man as Jim Craig took his farewell bow as a Celtic player as a triumphant winner at Hampden in the 1972 Scottish Cup final. Stein told the players that Cairney was quitting in the dressing room before the game and many say that was the inspiration for one of those vintage Hoops displays.

Hibs were battered 6-1 and Craig set up two late on with those trademark surges up the wing that had seen him become the architect of Gemmell's priceless winner in Lisbon. Jim had a brief spell in South Africa with Hellenic FC before returning to finishing his career with Sheffield Wednesday. He will always be remembered in my mind, though, as the educated man amidst the loveable rogues that were the Lisbon Lions. He was very high in my thoughts for the right-back jersey, as was a player who was my room-mate when I lived my life at the heart of the Hoops.

Jackie McNamara has such a quick football brain that he could play centre-half or central midfield and adapt to each changing role in a heartbeat. At full-back, he was like my old Arsenal team-mate Nigel Winterburn in that he used his intelligence to work out ways to combat the wingers he was facing. Winterburn knew, for instance, that when he faced Andrei Kanchelskis when we played Manchester United, he had to adapt. He wouldn't play right up against him because then they would throw a ball over the top and Nigel's lack of pace would be exposed by Kanchelskis, who was frighteningly quick. Instead he had this technique of getting in his eye-line and always threatening to close him down quickly when he received the ball. That made Kanchelskis think and it could nullify his pace; that's what Jackie did too. They were both clever footballers that way.

It's not always just about strength, pace and ability. Sometimes it's about awareness and intelligence and that was what kept Jackie at the top for so long. He was one of the cleverest footballers I ever played with and he was my captain and my room-mate. He looked after me at Celtic and he taught me a lot about the club. I'll always remember the love and respect he had for Tommy Burns. TB had been his manager in that season when Celtic lost just one league game but still didn't win the title during the Rangers nine-in-a-row years. Jackie had been blinding on the right with his best mate Simon Donnelly ahead of him and he thought that was the best football of the decade he spent at the Hoops. It hasn't surprised me to see Jackie and Simon move into management together at Partick Thistle, and I hope the board there have the courage and vision to stick with them. They are a legacy of their mentor Tommy Burns as football men and that can only benefit the fans at Firhill, who have always liked to see their football played with a bit of flair.

Jackie's best position was right-back in my eyes and he was magnificent in the Wim Jansen side that stopped Rangers from winning ten in a row in 1998 when he was voted Players' Player of the Year, the accolade that every footballer worth his salt wants to win. That's the one that means the most. Yet football is all about fate and timing and Jackie was a victim of circumstances when Martin O'Neill arrived at Celtic at first. The 3-5-2 system meant that we played with no full-backs, and in my early days at the club, with Agathe flourishing, Jackie became a squad player. He could have spat the dummy, sulked his way out of the club but that simply wasn't in Jackie's make-up. He stayed put, he bided his time and when we had injuries to the likes of Johan Mjallby and Joos Valgaeren he was back in the shake-up. He was a huge part of the League and Cup Double we won in 2004 and he felt he was back where he belonged.

It was a crying shame that Jackie's exit from Celtic was a bitter one as the club dragged their heels on his new deal and he gave his word to move to Wolves before a contract was finally offered to him. I know he was gutted about that and about the flak he took from some of the fans for leaving so soon after his testimonial against the Republic of Ireland. I really do hope that as time passes that sad end to his Celtic career is forgotten because Jackie deserves to be remembered fondly as one helluva player. I'll always recall this bond he had with Tommy Burns, the way they ripped the mickey out of each other. They were priceless. The only thing wrong with Jackie was his terrible taste in telly programmes. And the only thing he never did was get the TV remote off me at the Hilton on a Friday night!

When we are looking at the stars of the past it is always intriguing to assess the current players and wonder if one day they could feature in a book like this. Well, I'd say the present Celtic right-back, Adam Matthews, has a chance. He's a young kid with huge promise and I will always have a special place in my heart for any Welshman in a Celtic shirt. I feel he could impose himself on the game a bit more but he uses the ball well and he can be there for a long time to come. He has taken over from Mark Wilson, who was so unlucky with injuries in his Celtic days, he was a real steady player.

So for me, here in this position there were four key contenders that I thought of: Didier Agathe, who meant so much to my own side that reached the UEFA Cup final; Jim Craig who played alongside the legends of Lisbon; Jackie McNamara, who gave his heart and soul to the club and was so proud to be one of the lucky ones who wore the captain's armband; and, naturally, Danny McGrain.

Full-back is one of those slots you can make your own at a club. As a striker I was only ever as good as my last goal, that's how I felt. I was worrying about my movement, my touch, my heading and my finishing. At right-back you can break into the side and be there for a decade. If you can clip a ball into the striker, defend well, be an athlete, be organised to look along the line to your centre-halves, then you're made. Look at figures like Gary Neville, Stuart Pearce, Julian Dicks – these men are associated with one position and one club. But there's one man who was so good at right-back he made the Great Britain XI at LEFT-BACK. Meet Danny McGrain, my choice to tug on the number 2 jersey in my Celtic Dream Team.

That scenario came about in a studio at BBC Radio Five Live. When the station launched a quest to select their GB side, I was honoured to be asked to be on the judging panel because I knew they were constructing it in a unique way. They wanted strong, opinionated football men from each of the four Home International nations. I proudly represented Wales and we had ex-Scotland winger Pat Nevin, Nigel Worthington, the former Northern Ireland manager, and England legend Jimmy Armfield. It was a fascinating process because I found Jimmy such an interesting fella and he had a unique viewpoint on some of the older players I had heard my dad speak of. My old man was in awe of players like Wales legend Ivor All-church and the legendary Manchester United and England midfielder Duncan Edwards, who died so tragically in the Munich air crash that devastated the Busby Babes. Jimmy knew these guys, played with and against them and he was so knowledgeable.

The debates raged on that night and they were a joy to be part of and I'll always remember that when we selected United's Gary Neville at right-back Armfield was insistent that by hook or by crook we MUST find a way to get Danny McGrain in. He reasoned that Scotland had always switched McGrain to left-back because his Old Firm rival, Sandy Jardine of Rangers, was on the opposite flank. That opened the door for us and we decided against all the other names that we'd pondered and Danny was in.

Left-back might not have been his best position but I think a measure of how we regarded Danny is that we considered him to be in the same bracket as George Best. We decided we would create a position for him to make sure his name was in there. A GB XI without George Best was a ridiculous notion to us and it was the same with Danny McGrain, in our minds. I think that shows you where Danny stands as a footballer and it's amazing to think so many of the sixty-two caps that helped him enter the Scottish Football Hall of Fame were won when he was playing out of position.

But then again, Daniel Fergus McGrain is one of those guys who has been overcoming obstacles all his life. He grew up a Rangers fan, a Protestant born in Finnieston in Glasgow, and there has to be a real sense of sadness that his boyhood heroes didn't sign him. Not for Celtic, but for how you regard Scotland as a nation. A lazy scout wrongly thought his name meant he was a Catholic and in those days taboo for Ibrox. All that stuff just bewilders me. The religious aspect of football in Scotland before Rangers finally brought those barriers down and signed Maurice Johnston in 1989 is staggering to me. I have enormous respect for whatever people believe in, but to not sign a player because he is not a Protestant? I find that bizarre but that is why I steer clear of this subject in newspapers, pubs or if I am out socialising. I'm a footballer, not a religious leader or a politician.

Don't get me wrong, I am passionate about standing up for what I believe in. I could not have played for Team GB at the London Olympics, for instance, nor could I have sung 'God Save the Queen' because that is not my national anthem. That is the anthem for those who are from England or Northern Ireland. I am Welsh, my national anthem is 'Hen Wlad Fy Nhadau' (Land of My Fathers) and that is what I would belt out with all my heart. I'm a proud Welsh speaker and enjoy my work on S4C at home commentating in my native tongue on our Welsh Premier League games. The Republic of Ireland have their song and Scotland have theirs, the GB anthem should have been a different anthem from 'God Save the Queen' but that is an emotive issue with the nationalism that is involved there. That's pride in my country, not religion.

I know nothing about the Catholic–Protestant divide in the west of Scotland and I find it difficult to get my head around it so I don't even bother trying to understand it now. All I know is that Danny McGrain was a Protestant and so was Jock Stein, the greatest ever Celtic manager, so that makes a mockery of it all. Gers' loss in igoring McGrain was Celtic's gain, though, and Danny went on to play 679 times in the Hoops. He even has a real song in his honour. Not a terracing chant, mind, as back in 1996 a band called Big Wednesday had a single called 'Sliding in Like McGrain'. Bit special, that – I never had that. I'd have loved The Manic Street Preachers to sing a song about me!

When we sat in that radio studio at the BBC and recorded that programme a lot of names were thrown out there for left-back: Ashley Cole, Stuart Pearce, Tommy Gemmell – they were all in the mix. Yet always there was Mr Armfield insisting that McGrain just HAD to be there.

It's telling, I feel, that when Jock Stein took Scotland to the World Cup finals at España 82 it was Danny he chose as his skipper. He'd played under Willie Ormond in 1974, then been injured and was a huge miss for what turned out to be the debacle of Argentina 78 under Ally McLeod. In Spain, big Jock trusted Danny the same way Celtic did when he wore the armband for a decade, he was that sort of player. 'World-class' is a tag that is bandied around far too easily these days but it is one that Danny earned and deserved.

The big debate on that radio show was that we had to sell McGrain's worth to an English audience and he had never played any of his football south of the border. I think my passion for Celtic helped to sway the case here because I pointed out that he had World Cups in his locker and I knew what it took to be a mainstay for the Hoops season in and season out. There are those who refuse to examine your credentials if you haven't played in England but for guys like Danny and Paul McStay, playing for Celtic was the pinnacle of their careers. They COULD have played for Manchester United or Liverpool but they chose to stay in Glasgow and devote themselves to a very special club.

There were a few times during my Celtic days when I would come in to train with the reserves and Danny – who is still coaching the Development Squad at the club these days – would be in charge of the session. I was suspended and sent to work out with his boys to keep me sharp and those days were an eye-opener for me. Danny is sixty-two now so he was in his mid-fifties back then but there were times when he was tearing past me on the overlap! I just thought to myself, 'Jesus, this guy must have been some player in his prime.' He just has this love for the game and a real enthusiasm for football that I find runs through the veins of diehard Celtic men like Danny and the late and so much missed Tommy Burns. They lived for this game and they lived for the Hoops. I loved that about them.

Yep, Danny is the outstanding right-back in Celtic's history in my eyes and with seven titles, five Scottish Cups and two League Cup winner's medals, he has the honours to prove it. And although he didn't play in England I always found the big European games gave your season a huge lift. In my own career I was lucky enough to play for the likes of Arsenal and West Ham United but I'm just as proud of my days at Celtic and if anything my days in the green and white meant more to me. The reason is that with Celtic I was the main striker, whereas with the Gunners I was always playing second-fiddle to superstars like Dennis Bergkamp and Ian Wright. Sure, I scored in the European Cup Winners' Cup final for Arsenal when we lost to Zaragoza, but I came to appreciate just how a guy like Danny must have felt carrying Celtic's honour abroad and being a mainstay in the side.

If I hadn't been injured for the UEFA Cup final against FC Porto in Seville in 2003, Paul Lambert wouldn't have played that night. He ended up our skipper, but the European system was Chris Sutton in behind myself and Henrik Larsson up front. Lambo never thanked me for that back injury, now that I think of it! He owes me a lot.

Seriously, in the journey of this book, when it came to looking at players from eras before mine I liked to listen to the opinions of the guys who worked alongside the men I was picking. With McGrain, there was one word that kept on being repeated. Phenomenal. He had everything you require in that job and he redefined the role a right-back could play. You very rarely get a full-back like Danny who is fantastic both defending and going forward. Mind you, he was a creator rather than a scorer, as his total of just thirteen goals in those 679 games would tell you. He once famously said, 'The truth is that my bottle goes in the box, I just can't score.' That's honesty for you.

I love Chelsea's Ashley Cole as a left-back, for instance – defensively he is one of the best in the world in my book – yet when he crosses the halfway line he gets a nosebleed. He doesn't know what to do with the ball in some attacking situations. The polar opposite of that is Stuart Pearce, who could buccaneer forward and score great goals and he also defended like a monster. I remember playing for Arsenal against Nottingham Forest and Ray Parlour was playing wide-right for us. Ray just didn't want the ball that day because he was living in fear of Pearce. He felt that the minute he took a touch, Stuart would career in with studs raised and put him in the stand. Pearce was lurking there, living in his mind, haunting him, and I always felt Stuart had won the battle that day really before a ball had been kicked. At West Ham, Julian Dicks was the same – as capable of threatening the other goal as he was protecting ours. Well, I feel that Danny McGrain set the mould for players like that, he created the standard.

Lee Dixon at Arsenal was the best right-back that I ever played with – he just got up and down that flank and you always knew what to expect from him. He was defensively superb and he played in that great Arsenal back four of Dixon, Tony Adams, Martin Keown and Nigel Winterburn. They had David Seaman behind them between the sticks and to me that was a well-oiled defensive machine. Steve Bould would come into the mix later but whoever was in the heart of that defence knew they could glance to their right and rely on Lee. I respect him as a player and now as a pundit when you see him on *Match of the Day* on the Beeb. He's earned the right to criticise poor defending when he does his analysis, because he knew his job inside out when he had his boots on.

Lee was the best right-back I played with but the best I played against was the Brazilian legend Cafu. I remember facing him for when he was playing for AC Milan in the Champions League for Celtic. We lost 3-1 in Italy but held them to a 0-0 draw at our place. They were great games to be involved in and my abiding memory is that Cafu was still bombing forward in his veteran stage and I thought he was a thoroughbred footballer. Just like McGrain.

McGrain did play for Hamilton Accies in the final season of his career and, typically, won the First Division title with them. Yet it's the sight of him marauding up the right flank before delivering another killer cross in the green and white that always sticks in the mind. That's why Danny McGrain is in my Celtic Dream Team.

4

VOTING FOR THE LEFTIES

He could have been a male model or a professional golfer but my mate Gary Speed chose football and I'll always treasure the fact that he did. When I sat down to ponder the position of left-back for my Celtic Dream Team the same questions flitted through my mind. Who was the best I played with and against? That would tell me the qualities I had to look for before I settled on my choice.

Fact is that the best left-back I played with in my career wasn't even a natural in that position. He was a star midfielder who slotted in there because his manager asked him to for the good of his country and that summed Speedo up. Gary was equally strong on either foot but, in my eyes, he sparkled when he played left-back for Wales. Mark 'Sparky' Hughes was our manager in the Welsh national squad at a time when we had an embarrassment of riches in the midfield positions. We had the likes of Mark Pembridge, Simon Davies and Robbie Savage in there, and Sparky had a very simple philosophy: he wanted his best players in the starting eleven. That meant that he asked Gary to play at left-back because he was too good to leave out. I believed in Sparky's thoughts on that one, get your big-hitters on the park, get them playing, even if it is out of position. So that's how Gary Speed won fifteen to twenty caps in an unfamiliar position and it says so much about him that I would rate him the best left-back that I played with. He was terrific in our great run that took us to the brink of qualifying for the European Championship finals in Portugal in 2004.

That was the closest my country has come to making their first major finals since the World Cup in 1958. It was heartbreaking to lose 1-0 in that play-off to Russia because making it would have meant so much to so many of us, from Speedo to Ryan Giggs to myself. Gary was exceptional in that campaign, God rest his soul.

November 27, 2011, the day we learned that Gary Speed had committed suicide, was one of those moments in life you will always remember where you were when you heard the news. To be honest, I still can't comprehend it. Gary must have been in such an awful place to take his own life at the age of just forty-two. He had so much to live for and so many friends and yet he felt he couldn't reach out to any of us for help. That's what you just can't get your head around. It is such a tragedy.

I would rather not know now what lay at the heart of it all. I just want to remember my mate, this handsome man with the film-star looks, who worked so hard on his wonderful physique in training and was the sort of footballer any kid could look up to. He could have made his living doing photo-shoots for Armani, playing golf, whatever he wanted. He chose football instead and, believe me, he was one helluva player. I have lost my two grandmothers and had that grief to contend with earlier in my life, but Gary was the closest person I have ever lost. This was a man I got to know inside-out through over a decade of travelling the world with him in the Welsh squad. I looked up to him as a captain, he was our leader when I made my debut for Wales and he knew just how much that red shirt meant to me. Gary's eighty-five appearances make him the most capped out-field player in Wales' history and I think the ones he won in defence justifiably give me the right to class him as the best left-back I ever played with. He left behind a lovely wife in Louise and his two proud sons, Tommy and Eddie, and there are quiet times when I look at my missus, Sarah, and my four kids and my heart breaks for Gary's family. He will always be in my soul, he was one of the special ones I have met along the way in this life in football. I know that.

I think when you look at some of the best I played with in this position there might be that one little component missing. Nigel Winterburn at Arsenal, for instance, was such a terrific left-back and a guy I admired. But he barely scored any goals in his career, seventeen I think it was in twenty-two years at the top. I used to joke that it should be a national holiday if Nigel got one! When I think, though, of just how much we banked on Winterburn's class in my Arsenal days, it's bizarre to look back and see that he only won two England caps. Yet dig deeper and you see that he played in an era of Stuart Pearce, Tony Dorigo and Graeme Le Saux and that perhaps explains it. Nige was just unlucky.

I had a lot of time for Julian Dicks at West Ham United, he loved intimidating wingers with his skinhead and his menacing scowl, but he could play a bit too after he had put the fear of God into those players who loved the chalk on their boots. Ben Thatcher at Wimbledon was another left-back who loved a tackle and he is someone close to my heart because the bond we formed at that club meant he was at my bedside a lot when I was fighting for my life with the cancer.

I faced some terrific left-backs in my team when it comes to those that I played against but none can compare to Paolo Maldini of AC Milan and Italy. He was a thread running through my career – I played against him twice for Arsenal, three times for Wales and twice for Celtic.

I think when your club retires your number 3 shirt then you know you have been a pretty special player. Only Maldini's sons Christian or Daniel can potentially wear that jersey again. His dad, Cesare, was some player too and Paolo's kids already play in the Milan youth set-up – imagine the grief they'd get if they signed for someone else in that family? There is an argument that when Henrik Larsson left Celtic they should have retired the number 7 shirt and I would have my foot in that camp. But when Jimmy Johnstone and Kenny Dalglish have worn that jersey too, then there has to be a debate about that. Those are three of the greatest players to walk the earth, never mind play for Celtic. Their achievements for the club dictate that retiring the jersey would have to be in your thoughts.

Maldini was in the AC Milan team from seventeen to the age of forty-one when he hung up his boots and he has trophies coming out of his ears. Consider this for a record: five Champions Leagues, seven Serie A titles and

126 caps for Italy. Cast your eyes over that little lot and you realise just why I feel so honoured to have shared a pitch with the guy they simply called *Il Capitano*. He was a magical defender. I don't know what happens behind the gates at their camp Milanello where they train, but they are just rock-solid athletes.

When I played against Paolo I would embark on my usual journey to try and bully the guy I was playing against physically and it just didn't happen with him. They took no prisoners. I could ragdoll people in the English Premier League and smash my markers all over the shop in Scotland far easier than I ever could in Europe. Those men like Maldini were dedicated to their craft and they could stand up to the test of facing my physique. So I had to have a lot more in my locker than just brute strength to get the better of them.

I cherish the fourteen goals I got for Wales in my fifty-one caps in ten years in a red shirt because I found them all very hard to come by. International level is a step up in mind and body for a footballer and no one sums up the challenges you face more than Maldini. I had Ryan Giggs on my left and Craig Bellamy on my right at times, I had strike partners like Mark Hughes and Dean Saunders. There were no excuses – it's just that I think that one in three is a good strike rate at that level unless you are one of the truly special ones.

One of the best strikers Scotland ever possessed has to be the current Rangers manager Ally McCoist and he had nineteen goals in sixty-one caps. He had 355 goals in 581 games for Gers but, like me, he found that the challenges at European and international level against men like Maldini were daunting at times.

Left-back is a position that I looked at as a partnership in some ways: I knew Danny McGrain was landing my vote on the right and I had to find the player to complement him on the other flank. Tom Boyd is a player you could ponder for any of the positions across the back four in my Celtic Dream Team. It's a sign of his class that he could have been considered for both full-back positions and at centre-half.

Boydy wore his heart on the sleeve of that Celtic shirt with such pride – he was a terrific organiser on the pitch and had such a keen football brain. He was a terrific guy to have in the side. You look back at the deal that brought Tom home to Celtic from Chelsea and I think that just shows you how much fate has a hand in football careers.

Tony Cascarino had such a hard time in the Hoops and became the scapegoat for all that was going wrong at Celtic at the time. The club didn't pay too many big transfer fees back then but we'd shelled out £1.1 million for the big striker and the goals weren't flowing. It was natural that the flak would fly but the way out for big Cas remains a surprise when you look back at it.

Chelsea boss Ian Porterfield had Tom Boyd in his squad but for some reason he didn't fancy him as a player. I can't get my head round that one. Chelsea would shuffle their pack, change their system from a back four to a back three and the casualty would always be Boydy, who was trying to settle into life in London after making the £800,000 switch to Stamford Bridge from the Scottish Cup holders Motherwell in the summer of 1991. So when Porterfield was offered a swap deal with Cascarino going back south and Tom coming home to his boyhood heroes Celtic, he took it, and I have to say that has to be one of the better deals Celtic did in what wasn't the best spell in the club's 125-year history.

Boydy was one of those players that a manager could slot into any place in the defence then move on to your next dilemma knowing that you could rely on the man you had just selected to do his job in that position. Like Jackie McNamara, he was a humble, grounded and thoroughly decent Celtic man who lived and breathed the club and I always thought it was fitting when you look at footage of the 1998 title triumph. Take a glance at the moment the final whistle is blown on that 2-0 win over St Johnstone and you'll see the ball lies at the feet of Boydy. You can see just how much it meant to him to be the skipper of the team that stopped Rangers winning ten in a row and for all the pain he sometimes had to endure in his eleven years as a Hoops player, I know that day meant the world to Tom.

Boydy was at the club through years when they were often starved of success and at first that can seem puzzling when you think that he played alongside the likes of John Collins and Paul McStay, who I consider to be top-drawer midfielders. Yet when you scratch the surface of the teams they played in you see they were nowhere near as fortunate as me. I could look to a spine of stars who had been playing in the English Premiership and of course the phenomenon that was Henrik Larsson. Boydy, for the most part, could not. Celtic didn't have the quality in depth that we had when Martin O'Neill arrived and the purse strings were loosened. Simple as that. So it is testimony to a player like Tom and his devotion to the club that he treasures his time there so much and revels in the memories of the three titles he won. It was great that he was part of the Gaffer's Treble in 2001, the season before I arrived. Not many players in Scottish football history can say they were part of a clean sweep, but Boydy was.

My next left-back candidate, who was a Treble hero in 1969, is another man whose story shows you how much a club like Celtic gets under your skin. Jim Brogan signed for the Hoops in September 1962 but it took SIX YEARS for him to get his first winner's medal. He could easily have quit, gone elsewhere for a regular first-team game but elsewhere wouldn't have been Celtic so he stuck around and he reaped the rewards. Brogan's claims for the left-back slot are rock solid despite the fact he first came into Jock Stein's team as a sweeper. He'd been called into the side when John Clark was injured and he eventually staked his claim for a start the season after Lisbon, when his tough-tackling style alongside Billy McNeill helped the team to the title. By 1969 when the tackles were flying in big-style in the 4-0 Scottish Cup final win over Rangers, Brogan was becoming a commanding presence at the heart of the defence. His teammates always say with a wry smile that Jim loved a tackle, but you have to have more than that about you to look after the likes of Leeds United strikers Allan Clarke and Mick Jones as Brogan did alongside big Billy in the 1970 European Cup semi-final.

When Tommy Gemmell fell out of big Jock's good books, though, Celtic needed a left-back and Brogan was converted to the role with huge success. He put the shackles on the great Rangers winger Willie Henderson twice in a replayed 1971 Scottish Cup final and he made the number 3 shorts his to keep. In the years that followed, Brogan was vital, he became a mentor to the Quality Street gang of Danny McGrain, George Connelly, Davie Hay and Kenny Dalglish as Stein successfully injected fresh life into the team whilst still relying so heavily on players like Jim. Brogie might not have had the cavalier attacking flair or pace of Gemmell but history shows you that he racked up 332 games for Celtic, played a crucial role in stopping the nine-in-a-row and won seven titles, four Scottish Cups and three League Cups in his thirteen years in the Hoops. That's some record and fully merits his place on this list of candidates.

'Ten Men Won the League nah, nah, nah, nah!' I've been at more than one Celtic bash around the world when that song has been belted out to the tune of Boney M's 'Brown Girl in the Ring' and at first I wondered what it was all about. I soon learned the legendary tale of Billy McNeill's Bhoys beating Rangers 4-2 at Celtic Park with a man down to lift the title. Any player who was there that night lives on in the club's folklore and always will – guys like Andy Lynch. He was one of those players, like the current team's left-back Emilio Izaguirre, who suits the club's attacking philosophy. Lynch was a winger before he was converted to defence and he scored a Scottish Cup-winning penalty against Rangers in 1977 in an eventful stint in the job. Andy, whose son Simon went on to play for the Hoops as well, deserves a mention here. He was skipper at times, he had a real adventurous attacking spirit and he was in the team that beat the Gers and won the title with ten men. Good enough for me.

In the modern era I think Tosh McKinlay sticks out as a player who spent his career praying for the chance of a move to Celtic then made the most of it when the day of his dreams arrived. Tosh was staring at his thirtieth birthday when Tommy Burns paid £350,000 to Hearts to bring him to the club he had always supported. The former Scotland boss Craig Brown, who rated Tosh every bit as highly as TB did, called him 'The Specialist' because of the accuracy of the crosses he could whip in with that educated left foot. Tosh is the type of left-back I loved to play with. Alan Thompson and Steve Guppy had that same gift of being able to deliver a ball in at pace that you could go and attack, knowing a glance off the napper would do the trick. All the speed was on the ball, my job was to get in front of my marker and get the touch.

In the Martin O'Neill side I played in, I think it muddies the waters to look for a left-back because we didn't really play with one in that 3-5-2 system. The closest we had to one was Thompson, who was a wing-back really and shared that role at times with Guppy. He wouldn't go down as one of Celtic's greatest players but Guppy was one of those boys I loved to have in the team because he had such a great delivery and he could swing in the sort of crosses that I lived off. The fans might not remember him that much, but the likes of myself, Henrik and Sutty had so much time for him.

Thompson had what I love in a player, a big game attitude. When it mattered on the stages where some would freeze, Thommo would produce. Sure, he got a few Old Firm red cards but he had a lot of goals against Rangers too. Alan had that side to him that a lot of the great players have, a little edge of nastiness because they detest defeat. Wayne Rooney has it, Steven Gerrard has it, Paul Gascoigne had it. That edge could take them into tackles they might later regret but it wasn't ever something that I would chastise Thommo for. I loved the fact that he had that in him and he was a man I wanted in the trenches beside me when we were fighting for results at home and abroad. I loved him as a player and I thought he should have had far more than the one England cap he earned.

Looking back at it, England struggled for years to find someone to operate with bite and class on that left side. The answer was staring them in face, the problem was he was playing in Scotland and for a succession of England managers they just couldn't have that. What a joke. Even at Euro 2012 they were playing Ashley Young there and he was constantly cutting back onto his right foot. It's still haunting them. If my Wales mate Ryan Giggs had opted to play for England as he could have, then he'd have had 150 caps. They have always toiled there but, for me, Thompson was the answer and they ignored him. That it always puzzled me. He was an integral part of that 3-5-2 formation that Martin loved so much.

These days, of course, Celtic have a superb left-back in Emilio Izaguirre, who won Player of the Year in his first season after his bargain move from Honduras. You've got to salute the scouting network that brought Emilio here and he looked so good in that debut campaign. He was storming forward, getting up and down that left flank – he was just so exciting and he deserved all the accolades that came his way. Then came the inevitable when he was linked with a £10 million move to Manchester United: he breaks his leg at Pittodrie. And at the start of this season you had people wondering if he was believing his own hype. The fact is now that he faces a season of convincing the Celtic fans that he is not a one-season wonder. That might seem unfair when he has had such a cruel injury, but those are the demands of the jersey he wears now. Celtic have shown they can survive without him and Emilio now has a mission to get consistently back to the attacking threat he was in his first season.

Charlie Mulgrew has since followed him as Scotland's Player of the Year as a natural left-back operating at centre-half. What's to stop him coming back to the job he once had wide? So a few years from now Izaguirre might be in your thinking but this time round the likes of Jim Brogan and Tom Boyd play second fiddle to a man I think is the dominant choice at left-back. You see, in any exercise like this with Celtic your thoughts are dragged back to one team. Jock Stein's Lisbon Lions.

Tommy Gemmell has always carried such respect from those he played with and those he played against, and that's something he still has today. He is one of those mainstays of the Lions, a giant of a man with such a ready smile and a booming laugh. He loves life and I think he will always cherish the day he joined the Hoops from the junior club Coltness United back in 1961. For Tommy, coming to Celtic was such a pivotal part of his life and I realised that every time I met him at the Park. Jock Stein found players who wanted to live and breathe that place and I love that about that team.

His goal against Inter Milan means he is ingrained in Celtic's history and I think to not have him at left-back would have been seen as something of a sacrilege. I think the goal in Lisbon itself says so much about Tommy, big Jock and the Celtic way – to play with a bit of panache and attacking flair. I mean, look up the goal on YouTube like I did for this book and there is something you don't notice the first time you watch it. The ball is cut back to big Tam by the opposite full-back Jim Craig and then BANG! Goal from that rocket of a right foot. That shows the domination Celtic had in that game if both of the wide defenders can be that far up the pitch against a side of Inter's quality.

Look at the Inter coach Helenio Herrera, and that *catenaccio* style I spoke about earlier in the book. I think he would have SHOT his full-backs if they had been that far up the pitch! And what people forget is that Tommy went on to score AGAIN for Celtic in a European Cup final when the team lost 2-1 to Feyenoord in 1970. He is still one of only two British players to score in two different European Cup finals. The other? Puzzle it out, read on and I'll tell you at the end of the chapter.

I scored in a European final, the 1995 Cup Winners' Cup final for Arsenal against Real Zaragoza, but sadly it was in a 2-1 defeat. Tommy's goal was iconic, it dragged Celtic back into the match before Stevie Chalmers' winner and it is something he will always be remembered for. He nearly burst the net and I think that was the Gemmell trademark – he had some strike on him. When you think back, the balls were heavier in those days and they didn't deviate the way they do now. But when Gemmell hit a shot it stayed hit, firm and true.

I always marvel at the Lions and the way they create time for the fans, to tell their stories for the millionth time and pose for the pictures. They know how much they mean to the fans. Every one of that team from Billy McNeill to Bertie Auld to Tommy has that core of decency in them. They are terrific men and we won't see their likes again.

Gemmell was a different type of athlete from the modern day full-back in some ways. These days you might see an Ashley Cole or an Arthur Numan prosper. They are lithe, nimble guys and Tam was such a big unit at 6'2''. A daunting presence. For me, the man I would describe Gemmell like is Stuart Pearce of Nottingham Forest and England. Both were no-nonsense and if they had to put someone in the stand, they would. Pearce could get you double figures in goals each season and when he crossed the halfway line he played like a mid-fielder. That was Gemmell too. Pearce became such a prized commodity for club and country and, for me, Tommy paved the way for players like that.

As you will see as you read through my Dream Team, there are a few big characters with big personalities, and Tam was like that. We'd have had to separate grown men from scraps if we were given a penalty, that's for sure. Yet if I was the manager then it might well have been big Tam to take them, after all he scored thirty-one times for the Hoops from the penalty spot and only ever missed three.

I think Gemmell would bring a terrific attacking balance to my back four with Danny McGrain on the other side. I have left myself open to a debate with the 4-4-2 system in this, but I think the foundation of it, the defence, is as strong as you can get. It's funny, you know, so often with great players you look into their careers and there is one freak moment when they were slotted into a role that turned out to be made for them. With Tommy, he was playing for his amateur team Meadow Thistle in his usual position at outside-right when they were short of a left-back and he was dragged into defence. He never looked back from that moment and he actually signed his provisional forms with Celtic on the same night as the late, great Jimmy Johnstone.

I wanted my full-backs to be threats going forward, and in the modern day you need that and in the two I have picked there is such an added dimension in the team. These are not Steady Eddies, play-it-safe boys. They are bombing on. When I had settled on McGrain and Gemmell I sat in my garden in Swansea when we were doing this book and had a little daydream about how they would have liked it in my Celtic team in Martin's 3-5-2 formation. Well, I think they would have loved it because that system gave you such a licence to get forward. You could maraud on and know the insurance policy would be there behind you of the extra centre-half. Danny could race into attack knowing that behind him the Gaffer would have us drilled for the right-sided centre-half to shuttle across and cover. It was simplicity, but like most things Martin did, it worked. If both wing-backs go, in that system you can leave yourself exposed on the break, but McGrain and Gemmell were so intelligent as footballers they would have known that and they would have worked in tandem.

In our days I can always remember Johan Mjallby roaring at Didier Agathe, 'Go on, get up there, I'm here.' If Danny McGrain played for us on the road to Seville he would have spent three-quarters of the game in the opposition half.

That system is out of fashion now as so many teams play one up with players breaking off them to make the defences think, but what Martin did was mould that system to guys who suited it. As an assistant coach with Wales now, I like to look at the systems and how they work but, in all honesty, for every formation you come back to a home truth. The game is about good players and McGrain and Gemmell are certs in that category.

Tommy was part of a team that made the world sit up and take notice of Celtic and 1967 must have been such an incredible time for all those guys born within thirty miles of the Park. In that same year Tommy was part of the Scotland team that went to Wembley and beat England, the reigning World Cup holders, 3-2 in a thriller. My mates north of the border always tell me this means Scotland were the best team in the world for a while, and I'm sure big Tam wouldn't argue. By Christmas, the famous *France Football* magazine was rating Gemmell the sixth best player on the planet. That's unreal when you think about it, for a boy brought up in the Lanarkshire village of Craigneuk to reach those sort of heights.

And remember the question I asked earlier about the second of the two British players to score in two different European Cup finals? Well you may have already guessed it, but Phil Neal of Liverpool was the other man to hold such an honour.

Jock Stein – who often had bust-ups with Tommy, the big fella, over his off-field high-jinks or wages and all the rest of it – at one time called him the best left-back in the world and the Celtic fans were sure he was their choice in that slot when they voted for their Greatest Ever Team. I can't argue with those judgements and that's why at left-back Tommy Gemmell is in my Celtic Dream Team.

5

THE HEART OF THE HOOPS

Centre-halves. I've hated them, rated them, booted them, bullied them and respected the hell out of the best of them. And there are some positions in my Celtic Dream Team where I felt the choice was a stick-out but not centre-half. As you will read in this chapter, I felt there was one player who had to be there but the nod for the man alongside him had me scratching my head at times.

I thought of Mick McCarthy, who was such a down-to-earth scrapper and right up my street in terms of an honest, attack-the-ball centre-half. Davie Hay always tells me he was delighted to be given the £500,000 to sign big Mick from Manchester City because he'd been pestering the board for ages to give him the dough and then they finally coughed up. Mind you, they sacked Davie a few days later! Football, eh? There are times when you just couldn't make it up! Mick, though, was lucky in that Celtic then turned to big Billy McNeill as their next manager and no-one knows that central defensive beat better than Cesar.

Mick had the odd mad moment as a Celtic player, though, and flattening Falkirk's giant striker Crawford Baptie with a right hook to get himself sent off would be up there. Yet he was a rock in the 1988 Double side before the team hit the skids. McCarthy deserves his mention in this chapter because of the one quality I believe he has brought to every job he has had in his football career: his endearing honesty. He might not have been the best at coming out with the ball and playing passes but he would compete for every ball with every shred he had to give you. There's an old-fashioned part of me that loved the man-to-man combat against players like him when I was in my prime.

Mick the manager had his highs and lows, including that infamous bust-up with Roy Keane at the 2002 World Cup that led to Keane walking out on the Irish camp and coming home, but I think on the whole he is a players' gaffer who you would respect if you were working under him.

I pondered Paul Elliott, who brought such a lot to the Hoops in the early '90s having shown he had the class to play in Serie A with Pisa. The big Englishman was a cultured footballer who had a great mixture of steel and skill about him. I know he struggled with Scottish refs in his first season and picked up a whole string of bookings, but he must have been doing something right. After all, he won Player of the Year after that first campaign. Perhaps if Paul had stuck around at Celtic then the name of Elliott might well have been a serious contender for my Dream Team but in the end he went to Chelsea at the end of his second season for £1.4 million. Mind you, at least the club made some cash back on their investment –

which too often in the past hasn't been the case at Celtic – and the fans will always carry the memories of a genuine quality defender.

I admire Elliott's bravery in moving to Pisa in the first place. That took real guts. I had the chance myself to move to the Serie A at Perugia when Harry Redknapp walked into the West Ham training ground and told me one day, 'The Italians want you. The bid is there if you want to consider it.' Very quickly and firmly I said no because I would have hated training and playing in the heat with my colouring. I liked to train when I could see my breath making clouds of fog in the Barrowfield air, loved it when we had the rain jackets on and I could get a sweat up and the surface was greasy on top. Bottom line? The Serie A wasn't for a ginger man like me. Well, strawberry blond as I like to call it. Neil Lennon? He's a proper ginger!

Elliott had thrived in Serie A and he was excellent in the Hoops too. Sadly, though, like Paul McStay, he was in the Celtic soap opera in the wrong episodes. The team around him didn't match the skills and stature of a defender who was powerful in the air, quick over the ground and could play a bit too. The fact that Paul Elliott was Scotland's Player of the Year in 1991 in such a bang average Celtic team shows you what he had in his locker, but with the Hoops toiling he would always be tempted by overtures from down south and he left for Chelsea for £1.4 million without a winner's medal to his name. Celtic had just about doubled their money on him, but I still think that with Paul, whose career would eventually be ended by a bad tackle from my old Wales team-mate Dean Saunders, it's a case of what might have been.

Another candidate here has got to be Alan Stubbs, a player who I will always believe should have won more England caps than he did. I admire Alan both as a person and as a footballer. He came through the same hell of testicular cancer as I did with such courage but it's no sympathy vote to include him in the reckoning. He was a class act. The Celtic board sanctioned Tommy Burns lashing out a then club record of £3.5 million for Stubbsy from Bolton Wanderers in 1996, and I have always thought he was a quality defender. Stubbs could have easily fashioned a career in midfield, he was so comfortable on the ball and although injuries meant that TB never saw the best of him, Wim Jansen certainly did. He paired him with Marc Rieper in that 1998 season that thwarted Rangers for ten in a row and the big Scouser was brilliant. Alan twice fought testicular cancer, though after that and, like myself, those battles put any disappointment over how one's football career turns out into some sort of sane perspective. Some fans will look at the big fee paid for Alan and say it wasn't justified but fate played a cruel hand on Stubbsy at Celtic. That's all I know, and in my eyes he was some player.

Elegant on the ball is not, I would have to admit, a description of the next contender but it would never alter the big place Bobo Balde has in my heart as a footballer and a person. I would always freely admit that there are times when I still love simplicity in a defender. Clear the danger, fire that ball into Row Z if you have to. I'd hear the fans chanting, 'Bobo's gonna get ye!' as he came pounding menacingly towards an opposition attacker and I'd love it, to be honest. I remember the Dundee United striker Billy Dodds telling me that Bobo stood in front of him at the mouth of tunnel at Tannadice one day and the world went dark. He was bloody intimidating for strikers, even the brave ones like Doddsy.

Bobo should always be remembered for the role he played on the road to Seville and that UEFA Cup final in 2003. In the final itself he was eventually forced into a rash challenge that saw him sent off in injury-time in the 3-2 defeat from FC Porto, but, in my opinion, the big fella has nothing to reproach himself for. He gave everything he had to our cause. Yes, there were times when he could be rash or naïve in some tackles but you had to balance that against all the other crucial challenges he won clean as a whistle for us. His use of the ball wasn't the best but Martin always told him, 'You get the ball and then give it to someone else who can pass it!' Bobo never took offence at that, he didn't take it as a slight on his footballing ability as some might have, instead he simply recognised his own strengths and just did the job. And he could stop the best of them – look at Barcelona in the UEFA Cup at Celtic Park in 2004 when he was blinding in a 1-0 win.

I just felt that Balde was a fearsome machine and the three-man system we played at the back suited him down to the ground. I always saw Johan Mjallby, though, as one of the toughest players I ever faced – on the training field. There were times when the big Swede and I had to be separated at Barrowfield to stop us scrapping with each other. I remember one Friday morning training game where we were beasting each other in the air. It was a bruising confrontation each time a ball was slung in – I'd batter him; he'd clatter me. That competitive monster inside of me was just loving it. Eventually Martin sensed we weren't going to wise up or give an inch to each other until blood was finally drawn. He called a halt to the session and screamed, 'That's it! I'm banning the ball from going in the air. We can't trust these two lunatics, for God's sake we've got a ****ing game tomorrow!'

Mjallby would have run through a brick wall for Martin O'Neill and when I look now and see him cast as the calming influence alongside this firebrand manager in Neil Lennon I sometimes have a wry smile to myself and think that people are misjudging him. Believe me, big Johan is one helluva competitor and I have the bumps and bruises to prove it.

Mjallby could play a bit too but not as much as the 6'5" Slovakian stopper Stanislav Varga. Big Stan was some player and, to me, he was not as appreciated as he should have been by the fans. He could hit these great raking diagonal long balls that turned our 3-5-2 system from defence to attack in the blink of an eye.

Martin used different types of defenders, like Joos Valgaeren, and he could even draft the ever-reliable Jackie McNamara back in there, but I learned from him how to get the components right and make the defensive engine work. I see centre-half as the core of your team, whether it be a bully, a passer or a man who inspires you. And the best stopper I played with was a combination of all three of those qualities. When I was at Arsenal the trust George Graham showed in Tony Adams was displayed by the fact that he would allow the big man to take over the team talk in times of crisis for us. He was his on-field lieutenant, the man he believed in to get his message across on the pitch. He led by example and when I arrived at Highbury he was just this massive figure to me. Remember, I was a naïve nineteen-year-old kid from

Luton Town carrying a £2 million price tag, and he was the captain of England.

The answer to the toughest defender I played AGAINST often surprises a few people when I am on the road doing after-dinner speeches or my *Audience with John Hartson* shows that I enjoy so much these days. It's a question many fans pose and I always give that accolade to the same man – Roberto Ayala of Valencia. He wasn't the tallest of defenders, as he only stood at 5'10", but when you were in the wars with him it felt like he could jump seven feet tall every time a ball came in. He was like those Argentinian boxers you see contesting world titles at the top level – he lived to fight. He was a very physical competitor. Ayala starred in Italy for Napoli and AC Milan, but I think he will always be remembered best for his seven seasons at Valencia. I remember in the build-up to our games with them the press made a big play of the fact that his nickname was El Ratón, 'The Mouse'. I think he inherited it from the 1970s Argentinian forward Reuben Ayala, but it certainly had nothing to do with his personality – the guy was as brave as a lion.

Ayala played in three World Cups for Argentina, he won 115 caps and led his country sixty-three times, more than anyone else ever has. Only the legendary Javier Zanetti has more games for Argentina. That is the stature of the man I will always rate as the most difficult centre-half I played against. I wouldn't give out that compliment easily, not when I am a striker who played against the very best. I faced Fabio Cannavaro and Alessandro Nesta, Paolo Maldini, Steve Bruce, Neil Ruddock, Gary Pallister. The lot. I had to try and find a way to overcome every type of defensive obstacle in my time but I still rated the most testing as Ayala. Why? Well, as I say, the guy was scared of nothing, so I couldn't bully him. And when the ball came in to me in those Celtic–Valencia clashes I always had to think of how I could stop him from getting the better of me. I loved the jousts with him because he made me ponder how to use my physical advantages to win the battle.

I feel that the challenges I faced throughout a striking career at the top level on both sides of the border gives me a unique insight into choosing the centre-halves in this book. So here goes. When there was the debate to name the Greatest Ever Celt it was one that I followed with interest. I thought there was so much that went into winning that accolade, it wasn't just about how good a player you were, it was about how you conducted yourself, what you represented, your values as a Celtic man and as a Celtic player. There seemed to be two camps who were forceful in stating their cases, the more modern-day fans who supported Henrik Larsson and the older guys who wanted to see Jimmy Johnstone win it. Jinky was seriously ill with Motor Neurone Disease, fighting it so bravely, and he was such a prodigious talent no-one could argue too vehemently when the award went to a winger who captured everyone's hearts.

But me? I'd have had sleepless nights if I had been the sole judge and jury on that one but I've got to say that I would have given the nod to Billy McNeill. He is the Greatest Ever Celt in my eyes, the first British player to lift the European Cup, and that is something that no-one will ever be able to take away from him. Here's a stat I unearthed digging about for this book. Big Billy played 790 games for the club and he played every minute of every game he started. He was NEVER subbed – how impressive is that? His commitment to the club is unquestionable, whether it be as a player, a manager or a fan. Billy has been nothing but an inspiration at that club, and I think every captain Celtic ever has from now on in should strive to walk in his boot-steps. He set the benchmark for everyone else to rise to, he set the bar. McNeill was the epitome of what a captain should be.

I think as a group of men at work, whether it be in a newspaper office, a coalmine or a football dressing room, you look for a leader. McNeill was a born leader. They are in the autumn of their lives now, the Lisbon Lions, and every time a member of that team dies it brings such sorrow to the Celtic family because of what they achieved in the Hoops. Yet when one of these Bhoys is taken from us and you are at the funerals, as I have been, Billy always speaks with such dignity, humility and humour. All those players idolised their captain. Sure, Jinky and Bobby Lennox would have some fun with him and crack some jokes at the skipper's expense. Yet when it came down to it, they had such massive respect for him. Big Jock's right-hand man. He is a man who has my total respect, I worship the ground he walks on, to be honest.

I have met hundreds of the major figures in the game; I have been very fortunate. Yet I can honestly say that there is not one that I hold in more regard than Billy McNeill. I was lucky to have so many chats with him during my days at the club and since I retired we have shared a lot of social occasions together as columnists with the *Scottish Sun*. I think it is one of the greatest images in Celtic's history, McNeill up there on his own in the Estadio Nacional, hoisting the European Cup above his head. It means that everywhere he goes now he is lauded and every Celtic fan wants their picture with him. Yet he makes time for every one of them, always has a kind word, and that is the measure of the man. So Henrik, a great; Jinky, a legend. For me, though, the greatest was McNeill. That compliment won't sit well with such a humble man, but, for me, this is the skipper of my Celtic Dream Team.

Martin O'Neill used to have a pop at Neil Lennon if he got involved in a scrape that hit the front pages. I can hear it now: 'Listen, you, you're not just Celtic captain on the pitch. You're the captain off the pitch too. Strike that. You are Celtic captain when you're taking your wife for lunch. You are Celtic captain when you are SLEEPING. Look at Billy McNeill: now that's a Celtic captain.'

Martin wanted whoever carried that armband to live up to Cesar. That was the right policy for me. You are representing so many people around the world when you wear that armband now and Billy McNeill did that better than anyone else. It is fitting that the crowning glory of lifting the European Cup should go to a player and a man like Billy.

You know, it made me smile a little when Chelsea defied all the odds to beat Bayern Munich and lift the Champions League last season. They had spent almost £1 BILLION to get there. Big Jock got the job done with a team all born within thirty miles of the ground! That is a phenomenal achievement and at the heart of it all was Billy McNeill and John Clark. John has now been with the club for over fifty years – he's the kitman now, and Celtic remain in the fabric of his life.

When I was at Celtic Billy loved to come in for a cuppa and a chat with his old defensive partner and I got to learn what they built their double-act on. John swept up around Billy, that's how he described it. They called him 'The Brush', he tidied up the debris around the big man after he had breenged into a tackle or a header. Picked up the limbs and stuff! No, seriously, if I was picking a central defensive partnership I would have been sorely tempted to go for Clark and McNeill. What I have tried to do in this book, though, is pay homage to all the eras of Celtic's history and that's why I opted for another side-kick.

Billy was a centre-half who liked to go and compete, to win his personal duel with the striker he was up against. That's the type of stopper I respected as a target man. When McNeill was in his pomp in the '60s and the '70s, it was a time when referees would allow the use of the arm or the elbow for a defender to get the better of an opponent. It was accepted. You could still go through the back of a player to let the centre-forward know you were there. Big Billy always tells me with a knowing smile that he was an honest and clean centre-half, and from the footage I have pored over, he is telling the truth . . . to an extent! He wasn't dirty or nasty, but his vast European experience meant that he came up against the best around and he had to learn how to stand firm against them.

My new job as Wales assistant manager means that I study every game I watch now for the tactical nuances, I try to work out the systems, why a coach has set up his side in a certain manner. Well, I think when you look at the Lions you have to consider that Jock Stein was a master tactician who thought through every position in that team, and none more so than pairing McNeill with John Clark. Other teams may have had another destroyer beside Cesar, but not Celtic. Clark, a far smaller player, was more like a sweeper. That shows the manager was ahead of his time in that respect.

John is still such a part of the club now as the kitman, and I see him as in with the bricks. I used to love sitting and listening to his stories but at times you had to prise them out of him because he is such a humble character. Look through this book and the players I select and in those from the Lisbon side you so often see this knack that Jock Stein had of looking at them with a cold eye and seeing how their position could be tweaked to make them more profitable for the team. In John's case, that meant putting him in a sweeping role behind big Billy; he was made for it. You must have been a good sweeper if you end up with the nickname 'The Brush'!

So much changed after the 1965 Scottish Cup final for Celtic and that Hampden win over Dunfermline under big Jock ended eight years without a trophy and signalled a new dawn for us. If you want to know how much Celtic means to John Clark, look at the pictures of that day. He'd taken a horrible face knock and his jersey was literally soaked with blood – FIFA would have had him carted off these days. Instead, there he is, smiling through all the gore at the end!

Clark was a crucial part of the Lisbon Lions who won the domestic Treble and the European Cup in 1967 and his peerless partnership with McNeill makes him such a massive candidate to get the nod here. He was the first of the Lions to lose his regular slot in the team, to Jim Brogan from the Quality Street Gang reserve side, and that must have hurt, but John loyally stayed in the Hoops for three years after that. Clark and McNeill worked together when John was big Billy's assistant manager at Clyde and Aberdeen before John returned to the post he still has to this day as kitman at the club. I got an insight into what John meant to Celtic fans of an earlier generation than mine with Martin O'Neill. The Gaffer was a little bit in awe of John, which seems strange to say, but he was. He would always be asking Clarky to tell him stories about Jinky or the Lions, and it should be remembered that John once put the shackles on the great Pelé in a Scotland v Brazil match. He was that good.

Clark was at the hub of a defence that Stein clearly had so much trust in. I mean, think about it. In Lisbon they are facing the great Inter Milan and their coach Helenio Herrera and they bust down their defences with a left-back like Tommy Gemmell, being given the freedom to get forward and blaze in a goal. That shows you the belief big Jock had in those players and the way he built a team of legends. When Billy himself became Celtic manager, though, it was in an extremely challenging environment. McNeill had to face a Rangers side that was in the midst of the Souness Revolution. Funded first by the Lawrence Marlborough dynasty and then by his great friend David Murray, Graeme was being given fortunes to transform the Ibrox club. They signed Terry Butcher – who was then the England captain – and the England goalkeeper Chris Woods. Can you imagine Joe Hart and Steven Gerrard signing for Gers today? All Billy could do was cast envious glances from the other side of the city.

As a born and bred Celtic man, that must have been very hard to swallow – it wasn't anywhere near a level playing field. That's why I think one of the great achievements of the McNeill career at Parkhead as a whole is the

League and Cup Double he won as manager in the club's centenary year in 1988. To go from a player to a manager at the Old Firm is so very tough to do, and there has to be a worry gnawing away at those who do it. You have made yourself a legend with your boots on. Yet now there is the fear that somehow you will sully that by failing in the dugout. The problem is when the call comes, whether you are Billy McNeill, Lou Macari, Tommy Burns or Kenny Dalglish at Celtic or John Greig or Ally McCoist at Rangers, you simply cannot ignore it. This is YOUR team, asking you to lead them. It's the next best thing to playing for your boyhood heroes. Still, it took bravery, I feel, for Billy to accept the Celtic job on two occasions, and his greatest achievement was that Double, in my eyes. It was also won with such an exciting strike force, with players like Frank McAvennie and Andy Walker scoring priceless goals.

Billy was acrimoniously sacked by chairman Desmond White after his first spell as Celtic manager. It would have been very easy for him to nurse a sense of bitterness and turn his back on the club but he would NEVER do that. It's the measure of the man that what happened didn't rob him of his love for Celtic. He had won three titles, a Scottish Cup and the League Cup between 1978 and 1983 but he went in a bust-up over wages only to return as the gaffer again four years later.

Second time around the club again was being looked at to splash cash to match Rangers and Billy suffered as the board were accused of protecting the famous Parkhead biscuit tin and not giving their manager the funds to fight Souness. So, sure, on balance there have been more successful managers of the Hoops than big Billy, but my argument would be that he still enhanced himself as a Celtic man in the post. And from Burns to O'Neill to Strachan, every Celts boss in recent years has known they could turn to Billy for guidance and advice because he is always around the club.

Okay, it's a tough one, but my choice to partner Billy at the back walked into the Scotland Hall of Fame with fifty-seven caps and his heart on his sleeve. Roy Aitken. I think the simplest thing for me here would have been to simply select John Clark and take the core of the Lions as a pair. I chose not to for a few reasons. I think you have to look at all eras of the club's history and I also believe there has to be recognition for players who carried the Hoops through difficult periods. For me, big Roy was one of those players; he shed the tears as well as celebrated the triumphs. Again – like Billy as boss – he had to live through an era when Rangers were shelling out cash all over the place and try to rally his troops against a club that in all honesty had better players than Celtic did. Aitken is one of those players I would love to have in my dressing room as a coach, because you know what you are getting. Heart, commitment, soul, every shred he has, and also you know with him you could play him in a host of positions and get the same level of performance.

Punters and the press love nicknames and Roy's burly physique meant he was christened 'The Bear'. In full flight he'd be charging forward with The Jungle chanting, 'Feed the Bear'. Something else, that. Perhaps, though, it blinded some to just how good a footballer he was.

I believe that it is telling to look back on the maturity Roy showed from such a young age in a Celtic jersey. Think of the hype that would surround a Hoops player now if he were to score a double at Ibrox against Rangers to secure his team a 2-2 Old Firm draw at the age of just eighteen. That's what Roy did and the thumping volley that clinched a point from the late, great Johnny Doyle's free-kick was made all the better because the Gers fans were already celebrating a win, thinking the game was done.

If my goal against Liverpool was career-defining for me at Celtic then there is one game that sums up Roy Aitken for most Hoops supporters the world over. The night ten men won the league. When I look through the history of that famous match against Rangers it staggers me there was a TV strike and there is no proper footage of the goals. It's so sad because it is an iconic game and a story of footballing bravery and defying the odds against Celtic's greatest rivals. Any fan who was there or who has read the accounts since will tell you that Roy Aitken was the catalyst for that victory. He scored one and made two and I think that was when he secured a place in the club's folklore.

One of the outstanding times of Roy's later career was as a warrior in the centre of his country's midfield at Italia 90. That showed he could operate so well there at the very highest level as his side came back from a typically Scottish nightmare in the opening defeat against Costa Rica to beat Sweden and go so close against Brazil. Me, though? I admired Aitken, the swashbuckling centre-half, and I think he would have made a brilliant partner for McNeill. Big Roy could mix it alright, but I think his passing ability was under-rated. He could spot a ball out of defence and I just look at the mix I have created in the heart of my defence here and think I have got it right. I mean, if you were an opposing manager and you looked at our back four on a Saturday afternoon at Celtic Park and it read McGrain, Aitken, McNeill (captain), Gemmell, would you be thinking anything but, 'Dear God, how do I break that lot down?'

I have chosen a lot of players in this side who I see as driving forces, the kind of players I always loved to share a dressing room with. Aitken fits the bill there, and I used to love listening to my Celtic pals tell me the stories of the final-day title triumph in 1986. All Hearts had to do to clinch a historic championship was win up at Dundee, while Celtic had to crash in the goals at St Mirren and hope for the best. The Jambos blew it, losing 2-0 at Dens, and what followed at Love Street was a memorable chapter in the Hoops' history, as Aitken roared his side on to a 5-0 win that sealed the crown.

Days like that sum big Roy up and that's why for me he has just edged the likes of Tom Boyd in my selection. I think Tom is one of those players you could have looked at for either left-back or centre-half, he was equally comfortable in either role, as a tale of seventy-two Scotland caps shows. Tom is another of those men I met in my days in Glasgow who is simply steeped in the club, who understands its values and lives by them. It's great that he is still involved in the coaching set-up there with the Under-17 side because those are the types of people who should be moulding the next generation of Celts.

This was a tough one. John Clark weighed so very heavily on my mind, but I think I have the correct combination to strike fear into the heart of any front man. Cesar and The Bear. Billy McNeill and Roy Aitken are in my Celtic Dream Team.

6

THE ONE AND ONLY

He threw his shirt at Jock Stein when he was subbed and lived to tell the tale after the big man chased him down the tunnel. He taunted Real Madrid and the Bernabeu stood as one and roared 'Ole' every time he teased and tormented their defenders. He haunted Rangers on the way to inspiring Celtic to nine in a row, yet their fans stood on the street to honour him when he was laid to rest on St Patrick's Day in 2006. Those three stories sum up James Connelly Johnstone. Otherwise known as Jinky, a true footballing genius.

When we set out on this project with the publishers we drew up a plan to take you through the journey of these pages. Build up to the selection in each chapter, name the other contenders, stoke up the suspense. Well, I'm sorry, but on the right side of any Celtic Dream Team there can be no debate. It has to be the one and only Jimmy Johnstone. A man I was lucky enough to get to know in moments that I will treasure for the rest of my life.

I will always remember the times I met Jimmy because I was genuinely star-struck and that doesn't happen to me often. I've played with and against some of the best around in this game. Jinky, though? That's a different matter. He would give me little bits of advice about how to pull away off my marker better and find that vital yard I needed to score the goals that were my lifeblood as a striker. I would walk away from those conversations feeling so humble and one thing that sticks in mind is that it was always about him praising me. Jimmy never really talked about himself or what he had done in the game.

Every player needs heroes to look up to when they are growing up. Mine was Ian Rush. He played for Liverpool and Wales and as a kid that was all that I ever wanted to do. I love Celtic now but I would never patronise anyone by saying I grew up running round the streets in the Hoops as some players do, I was a Swansea lad and a Reds supporter. Jimmy's hero was the late, great Sir Stanley Matthews and he'd be out there every night copying the great man's techniques and dribbling in and out of empty milk bottles on the street. Jimmy McGrory was the Celtic manager who signed Jinky but if you look at the history it tells you that the wee man toiled at first.

Jinky played in the Scottish Cup final and was the star man in a 1-1 draw against Rangers only to be dropped for the replay amidst fury from the fans, who insisted powerful chairman Robert Kelly was picking the team for McGrory. Celtic lost the rematch 3-0. Jinky was in the doldrums but the arrival of Jock Stein meant a different Celtic – and a rejuvenated Johnstone. Again, though, it is worth reflecting that Jimmy was not included in the team for the 1965 Scottish Cup final win over Dunfermline that is seen as the birth of the Stein era at Celtic. The two would in the end have a tempestuous relationship that saw Stein inspire Jinky, for all his off-field high jinks, into some unbelievable performances when he crossed that white line in a green and white jersey.

I love it that for all the greatness they would achieve together, for all the cajoling, the punishing, the training and the goals, the highs and the lows, the laughs and the bust-ups they would have in Jinky's time in the Hoops, one thing stood true from the start. He had to prove himself to Stein to win a starting jersey. He did it, and by the time Celtic won their first title in twelve long, hurtful years at Motherwell in May 1966, Johnstone was one of the first names on big Jock's team sheet. It goes without saying what Jimmy brought to the Hoops, to be voted the Greatest Ever Celt on that glittering night in 2002 when the fans made their choice for an accolade every Hoops player would have cherished. Jinky won that and it was God's will that he was still alive as he battled the Motor Neurone Disease that would claim his life at the age of just sixty-one and be there with us to accept it.

He was the type of player who needed a ball for himself. They should have given his team-mates another one to play with and left him to it. He was so difficult to dispossess and the Lisbon Lions told me there were times when they would literally STOP during games just to watch how good he was. I savoured every video I could watch of him in action like the superb 'Lord of the Wing' and it nags at me when I speak about him down south that the name of Jimmy Johnstone is not revered the way that it should be.

There are scenes in that DVD that sum Jinky up for me, the footage of his goals from a 2-2 draw at Ibrox on

May 6, 1967 that clinched two-in-a-row against a raging Rangers. He has his socks rolled down running at defenders, the mud is clawing at his boots as the rain pours down. He dances away from tackles and then he fires this thunderbolt of a shot from distance into the top corner with his weaker LEFT foot. Only the great ones do things like that.

The English wouldn't put him up there with the likes of George Best or Diego Maradona but they should, in my opinion. The problem for them is that he played the major part of his career for Celtic and Scotland. The spells at San Jose Earthquakes, Sheffield United, Dundee, Shelbourne and Elgin City in the four years after he left Paradise mean little in the context of his football life. Jinky was a Celtic man.

In the wake of that career-defining European Cup final win over Inter Milan in 1967 it would have been easy to pack the tools away. They could have gone on the lash and celebrated becoming legends in their own lifetimes. Instead the Lions went to Madrid and Jinky tormented the great Real side in Alfredo di Stefano's testimonial match. This way and that, beating men for fun, a virtuoso performance that left the Santiago Bernabeu Stadium standing in his honour as the Hoops won 1-0 and confirmed themselves as the cream of the continent. In that glory year there was recognition of a sort for Jimmy when he finished third in the European Footballer of the Year behind Hungarian legend Florian Albert, who starred for Ferencváros, and Bobby Charlton of Manchester United. I would never diminish the contributions that year of men of that stature, but would it really beat what Jinky did for Celtic? Clinching the league, inspiring his team to becoming the first British side to win the European Cup, having the Bernabeu eating out of the palm of his hand as Celtic beat Real Madrid in di Stefano's benefit match?

They said Real tried to sign Jimmy after the game – truth is he would have walked into the team there – yet he never truly got his name on the world stage. Still, every Celtic supporter on the globe has Jinky in his heart and that would have been enough for the wee man. I know that. If he had signed for Manchester United, as he could have as a thirteen-year-old kid, were it not for the intervention of a shrewd Celtic scout called John Higgins, then he would have been known to every football fan on the planet, but it shouldn't change the perception of him in my eyes. He was a footballing phenomenon.

Before I came to Celtic I knew the name Jimmy Johnstone but I didn't know the legend, I didn't truly recognise just what he achieved in a green and white jersey. I will always treasure the fact that I got to meet Jimmy and he was such a humble man as he fought that horrible disease, a guy who loved a beer and a night out with the fans. That bond with the supporters is a thread through the lives of all of the Lisbon Lions. There are times now when it is difficult to get a Celtic player to attend a function because of the autographs and the pictures. Some players don't like it, but the Lions know their place. They sign every piece of paper and pose for every picture.

Jinky was a man of the people, who played for the people – that was the way I saw him. He played to put a smile on the faces of the supporters. He would stand for hours outside the Park talking to fans – some players now can't get into their cars quick enough to get away, and that's a shame. Jock Stein was a tactical genius but I think he knew that Johnstone was one player he didn't need plans or formations for. He was like the Paul Gascoigne of his time, you just let guys like that go and play. For those special ones you cannot take away the sheer enjoyment that they get out of beating men and being creative. From Maradona back in the day to Lionel Messi at Barca now, they are allowed to run the show and I think big Jock knew that was the way to get the best out of Jimmy too. There was no point in trying to bemuse him with talk of tracking back and strangling him with discipline. Celtic Park was just like the school playground to him and he was back nutmegging his mates and making them look daft. The only difference is, it wasn't jumpers for goal-posts.

I was a brute of 6'2" and nearly sixteen stone, but look at Jimmy and he looks like a waif who you could easily muscle off a ball and kick out of a game, doesn't he? Forget it. There is a way of playing football at the club I love, the Celtic way. For me, Jimmy Johnstone is the embodiment of that. Fans love mavericks who entertain them and Jinky was the man who created the brand. I mean, who else could be lifted to new heights by his fear of FLYING but Jinky. He was scared stiff of aeroplanes and many say his greatest hour in a Celtic jersey came in a European Cup clash with Red Star Belgrade at our place. Big Jock knew the wee man didn't want to get on that dreaded plane for the second leg and he told him that if he could get the side in front by enough goals he would be left at home. Jinky duly either scored or set up four in the second half and the Hoops won 5-1. The Yugoslavians were desperate to see Johnstone in their stadium for the return match but his manager was as good as his word. Jimmy stayed home.

In my time at Celtic there were players who thrilled the fans at times with the likes of Shaun Maloney and Aiden McGeady. They were always encouraged to play with their natural flair because the club loves that type of footballer. I feel Aiden has gone on to show what a good player he is after his £9 million departure to Spartak Moscow in what was a brilliant piece of business for Celtic. Russia is a helluva adjustment to make but he's done that. His final ball can be a flaw, however, and that is a weakness for so many wingers.

Ryan Giggs, for all his majestic skills, could never match the delivery that David Beckham had from the other side in their Manchester United heyday. Beckham, though, never had the pace to terrify defenders that Ryan had. It's very difficult to find the whole package in wide men. Well, Jinky was the whole package. He even famously scored two HEADERS against Rangers – and they were both winners. That's unreal for a player of his height of around 5'2''. Look, though, if you win the Greatest Ever Celt ahead of absolute world-beaters like Kenny Dalglish and Henrik Larsson, then you have a right to consider yourself as special.

I used to watch Jimmy make a fuss of kids who came to shake his hand and marvel at the way he treated his own folk. He truly was a working-class hero in a way that modern-day footballers can't really be. Nowadays they are glimpsed behind the windows of blacked-out Jeeps and the gates of training complexes and can seem so distant to the punter on the street. That wasn't Jimmy, he was always the life and soul of the party and he loved a night out. Who else could record a duet singing 'Dirty Old Town' with Jim Kerr of Simple Minds and belt it out so well there isn't a dry eye in the house? Jinky simply had star quality and the fans forgave him his flaws because they relished his genius.

The closest thing to him now? Messi – I look at the Barcelona and Argentina superstar and see shades of Jinky. Messi goes past people as if he is a fifteen-year-old kid player against eleven-year-olds in his little brother's class at school. He beats people as if they are not there and Jinky was the same.

Bravery can mean so many different things in football. For me it often meant getting across the front post and throwing my head in where the boots were flying to try and score a goal. For Jinky it meant getting kicked black and blue – like he did in that infamous 1974 European Cup semi-final clash with Atlético Madrid at Celtic Park – and getting up to take some more. The newspapers showed pictures of the brutal treatment meted out to Jinky and his legs were covered in cuts and bruises as the animals of Atlético had three sent off on a shameful night. Before the second leg Jimmy received death threats but still played as the sickening Spaniards won 2-0.

The courage he showed was also summed up by the way he would constantly demand the ball in tight spaces, knowing defenders who towered over him were coming to hunt him down. Look at the Leeds United games in the 1970 European Cup semi-final when Norman Hunter and Jack Charlton would have had his name on their list but they could never kill his spirit no matter how hard they hit him. And he could handle himself alright. Watching the tapes, you can see that once or twice his temper snaps and he has a go back. I remember him having a laugh with Henrik Larsson about that because Henrik could get his arms up to protect himself and if he needed to be nasty in the tackle then he could be. Most great players have that edge to them; they are not shrinking violets. They have massive hearts and in Britain they often have a determination that has seen them overcome the prejudices we as a race carry about smaller players to become stars. Look at my own country, Wales, and the impact made by players like Mickey Thomas, Brian Flynn and Craig Bellamy. They would cause a fight in an empty house, that lot!

I loved to laugh at Jinky's stories when we met and he educated me about how to get a rowing boat and go sailing at Largs when you have had a few pints. I don't think his timing doing it when he was on Scotland duty was the best, right enough. Oh, and he forgot the oars. Now I know his manager would have been furious at the time but when you think of that caper I defy you not to crack a smile even if you disapprove of the lack of discipline.

I was privileged to be at Jimmy's funeral when they lined the streets of the east end of Glasgow for him before he was laid to rest at Bothwell Park Cemetery. Sir Alex Ferguson, Walter Smith and the great and the good were all there – you would have thought this was the death of a Prime Minister. For miles and miles they stood at the roadside to pay their respects on the route of the funeral cortege and it was staggering. It was like a European night at the Park itself, it took my breath away to see the amount of people so deeply affected by his death.

If I had to look at someone I have played with in that right-sided role and give the accolade of the best one it would go to Craig Bellamy during my fifty-one caps with Wales. He is a feisty player but someone who carries pride and desire into whatever team he plays for. I didn't agree with his decision to play for Team GB at the London Olympics. As a proud Welshman I'd have told them to stuff it, but he still gave every shred he had in the matches. If you want to see how he is regarded as a footballer then just look at some of the managers who have signed Bellamy, from Graeme Souness to Kenny Dalglish. They know a player.

I have played against some real belters in that position too. David Beckham, Cristiano Ronaldo and Ronaldinho. How do those three sound? Picking one of those for the best team I have played against is so difficult. Yet when I played against Ronaldinho for Celtic against Barcelona he was without question the best player in the world at that time. Joos Valgaeren did a great job man-marking him and I remember Martin O'Neill's team talk. He said, 'Listen, Joos, if he goes to the toilet you better be beside him in the cubicle holding the toilet roll.' Joos carried it out to the letter! He marked him out of the game, we drew 1-1 in the Nou Camp and I scored on a Champions League night I will never forget.

He drifted all over the place that night and the reason I have included him in this chapter hailing a maverick is that on a pitch in my career he was the closest I have seen to someone playing in the spirit of Jimmy Johnstone. By that I mean that every time Ronaldinho got the ball he tried to make something positive happen. He didn't believe in the simple pass to the left to the nearest team-mate, for the sake of keeping the ball.

Look, there are so many techniques you need to make a great team. Neil Lennon, for instance, was crucial for my Celtic team because he never gave the ball away but equally he was never going to make you a goal with a pass through the eye of a needle either. The Xavis and the Iniestas have the vision to try and make that killer ball. They might give it away doing it but they are capable of completing it. The Jinkys and the Ronaldinhos are the positive types who want to nutmeg you and make something happen.

This was an easy choice for me to make but there are two players I have a soft spot for who deserve a mention even though they would confess they couldn't argue with my selection of Johnstone for this role in my Dream Team. The first from some of the best days of the '80s for the Hoops is Davie Provan and he is man I don't just admire as a player but now also as a football columnist in the Sunday edition of the *Scottish Sun*. Davie upsets fans from Rangers – and Celtic – with his forthright views and I think he shows a lot of courage shooting from the lip every week. His arguments are reasoned and you might not agree with his standpoint but you will always see the logic behind what he is saying. That's why I look forward to his column every week. In my opinion, if you are not lucky enough to be employed by Celtic then you have a right to make a living in the media. If Neil Lennon wasn't the manager of Celtic then I am sure he would be working for the *Scottish Sun* or the *Daily Record* commenting on the game.

If you're as opinionated as we all are then you want to have your say and the nature of the beast in the tabloid arena is that it is going to make big headlines. That's what you are paid for, not to sit on the fence. You have to tell it as it is, you have to be honest with yourself and the sports editor you are working for. Otherwise, in my eyes, you are stealing the fee. I never did that as a player and I refuse to do it as a newspaper columnist. I enjoy a friendship with the Head of Sport, Iain King, who has helped me with this book but that has not gained me contracts five years on the spin since he took over. It's my views, at times outspoken, and my analysis and intelligence I have for assessing footballers and football matches.

At times I have upset people in the Celtic family but I can sleep at night knowing that I have given an honest opinion, and if people don't like it then I am sorry. If I am not allowed to voice my opinion as strongly as I want to then there is no point in me doing the column. I refuse to be mealy-mouthed and patronise people, it's not me and it's not Davie Provan. He has a big set of balls to do the job the way he does it both in the *Scottish Sun* and on Sky Sports. He is fearless in his views and I have a lot of respect for him for that. He puts himself out there to be debated every Sunday afternoon in the pub or on the radio. His column is never dull.

Provan the player was a winger with pace who could take people on and then pick out a great final ball. I've heard him criticise Aiden McGeady once or twice about that killer cross because he felt Aiden lacked it and he had a point there. Davie's final ball could be spectacular in his heyday and that failing of McGeady grated on him. Provan had delivery, he could pick them out and like a lot of Old Firm players this was first noticed when he sparkled AGAINST them – in Davie's case for Killie against Celtic when they knocked the Hoops out of the Scottish Cup in 1978.

Davie's move to the east end of Glasgow six months later was for a then Scottish record fee of £125,000 and he went on to more than justify that in the years that followed. To be honest, being one of the star men the night ten men won the league against Rangers would have been enough for most fans!

These days Davie's hair is shorn into his head but back then he had this brilliant perm and a style all of his own, with the socks rolled down to his ankles, the little jinks, the deliveries into the box every striker dreamed of. He was something else. One goal I love to look back at is his free-kick in the 1985 Scottish Cup final. Do you know why? Because it took such bottle to swerve that one past the Dundee United goalkeeper Hamish McAlpine. We were losing that final, and that's not in the script for Celtic at Hampden, and the pressure becomes unbearable when you are a goal down in a game like that and you need someone to dig you out of the s***. That's what Davie did that day and after it you could just sense the late winner coming. It did, thanks to Frank McGarvey.

Davie's loss to the game after he was diagnosed with ME was tragic and I'm told his testimonial game against Brian Clough's Nottingham Forest was a really emotional occasion with Kenny Dalglish guesting for the Hoops in the middle of the Centenary Double-winning season. Davie's raids down that wing and the greatness he showed in the Hoops mean that in the years to come he had earned the right to have a pop at Aiden McGeady if he couldn't deliver a telling ball. Davie Provan played 303 times for Celtic, he scored forty-two goals and set up barrowloads more. He deserves his place in this chapter on the same pages as Jinky.

The other guy I loved in a Celtic jersey was Paolo di Canio, and he must have loved the shirt too – he kissed the badge enough! Seriously, one of the sad things was that I never got to play with Paolo. West Ham United actually bought him with the money they got for me from Wimbledon. In fact, out of the £7.5 million they got for me, Harry Redknapp went out and he spent the lot on midfielder Marc Vivien Foe, who would later die on the pitch playing for Cameroon, God rest his soul, the left-back Scott Minto and Paolo. So I missed di Canio at Celtic and I missed him at West Ham and he is one player that I would have loved to have played with. I think I would have been good for him and he would have been good for me because he was a goal-maker.

As much as he could score goals, I always saw him more as a creator. He was also a player who got better with age and looked after himself superbly well. Some players are like fine wine and mature like that, and Teddy Sheringham and Kevin Phillips are two other great examples. Henrik Larsson always told me he was a better player at thirty-two than he was at twenty-two. He was a fitness fanatic who watched his diet and was a beast in the gym and at training. It was like that with di Canio, who was in the later stages of his career.

It was typical of Tommy Burns that he should sign a player like Paolo for Celtic, he could make the ball talk. He was brilliant in possession and he had an edge to him, flaring up on the training ground and even once, in his Sheffield Wednesday days, hilariously pushing over the ref, Paul Allcock. I played against di Canio many times and the only time we played together was in the Tommy Burns testimonial when we shared the same pitch and had a few laughs about the Hammers and 'Arry. He was a gentleman and I loved that day.

You often find that the players with flaws in their character are the best fun to be around. With myself I have Rangers fans who think I am this horrible Celtic beast who battered their defenders around, then they have a pint with me and find out I'm actually quite a nice, humble fella! They are staggered, because in Glasgow many people judge you by the colour of the shirt you wore playing football. Yet once they know you a little bit they realise you are very different from the public perception and Paolo is like that.

When you consider that Paolo only played one season in the Hoops his impact was huge but his £1 million capture from AC Milan was such an inventive signing from a manager who just loved attacking players like di Canio. With Pierre van Hooijdonk, Jorge Cadete and Andreas Thom all in the side too, defence was never going to be their strongest suit but there are so many fans who remember the games when those four clicked as if they were yesterday.

Bottom line, though? In football's mean city you have to beat the Rangers and the season Paolo was at Celtic TB's side lost all four league encounters and even when the Italian scored a penalty and they beat Gers 2-0 in the Scottish Cup quarter-final they went on to lose to First Division Falkirk in the last four.

When Tommy was sacked by Celtic I think Paolo saw that as a way to manoeuvre his own exit and he was soon off to Wednesday in a £4.5 million deal that also brought

Regi Blinker the other way to the Hoops. Paolo tainted his legacy, but I think if you look at this on pure ability and explosive impact on the club then he bears mention here.

With Wales I came agonisingly close to the Euro 2004 finals but never made it onto the big stage of a major tournament with my country. Neither did Giggsy, neither did George Best with Northern Ireland. I know that by the time he got to Germany 74 with Scotland, Jimmy was not at the peak of his powers but he still got there and it must have been a major regret when he came to hang up his boots that he wasn't used in three games in the finals. To look back and think that a player of Jinky's calibre only got twenty-three caps for Scotland is a travesty. They say he suffered dog's abuse from the Rangers fans when he turned out for Scotland because they felt Willie Henderson should have been playing. All I know is that his country could have got so much more out of him.

In the summing up of this great footballer, I think the most telling thing is that Jock Stein put up with the off-field antics and the problems Jinky could sometimes bring him because he trusted him so much as a player. Their worst clash came in October 1968 when Jimmy was subbed in a home game against Dundee United and hurled his jersey at Stein in a fit of fury. It hit his manager in the face and Jinky hot-footed it down the tunnel with his seething gaffer in hot pursuit! He recovered from that blunder the way he would others, by convincing big Jock of his worth to Celtic. It was fitting that Jimmy's testimonial at Celtic should have been a joint match with his great pal Bobby Lennox against Manchester United in 1976. The Hoops won 4-0.

© SNS GROUP

THE BIG MAN … Jock Stein's eye for the little tweaks that could change a player's career was critical

© KENNY RAMSAY/THE SCOTTISH SUN

BATTLES LOST … I had the bottle to challenge Martin O'Neill – but I never won a single one of those fights!

© KENNY RAMSAY/THE SCOTTISH SUN

PRIZE GUYS … with the Gaffer picking up Manager and Player of the Month awards. He made a habit of it

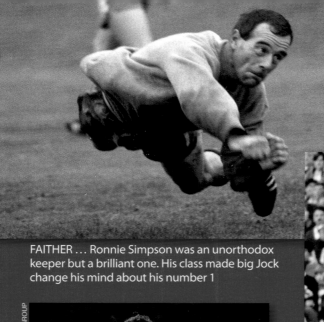

© SNS GROUP

FAITHER … Ronnie Simpson was an unorthodox keeper but a brilliant one. His class made big Jock change his mind about his number 1

© SNS GROUP

DANNY BHOY … McGrain was a truly world-class right-back – I even picked him in a GB Eleven at left-back

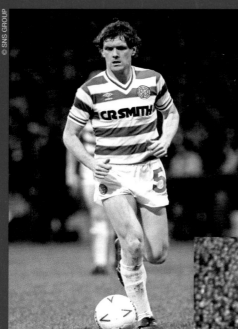

© SNS GROUP

FEED THE BEAR … many saw Roy Aitken as a midfielder but I loved to see him storming out of central defence

HAIL CESAR … big Billy McNeill led the Lions magnificently, and he remains the head of that band of brothers today

BIG TAM ... Tommy Gemmell scored in two European Cup finals for the same club, only one other British player has done that

WORKING-CLASS HERO ... Jimmy Johnstone was a true footballing genius, yet I discovered he was such a humble man who just loved the Celtic fans

© SNS GROUP

THE MAESTRO … Paul McStay deserves so much respect for sticking with Celtic through some dark days for the club

THE GENERAL … Bobby Murdoch made a habit of lifting trophies in the Hoops, then he taught Graeme Souness how to be a player!

© SNS GROUP

LEMON FIZZ … only Mr McGrory has scored more Celtic goals than Bobby Lennox, a true gentleman and a legend in my eyes

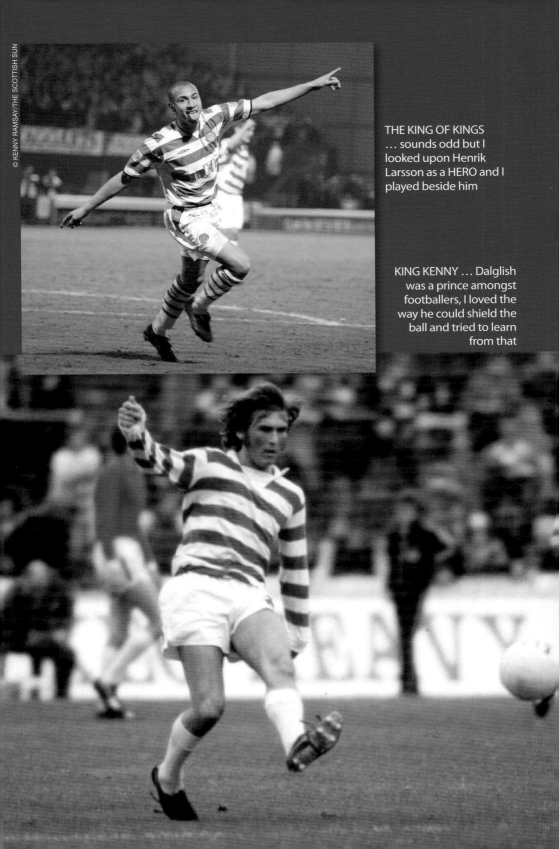

THE KING OF KINGS
… sounds odd but I
looked upon Henrik
Larsson as a HERO and I
played beside him

KING KENNY … Dalglish
was a prince amongst
footballers, I loved the
way he could shield the
ball and tried to learn
from that

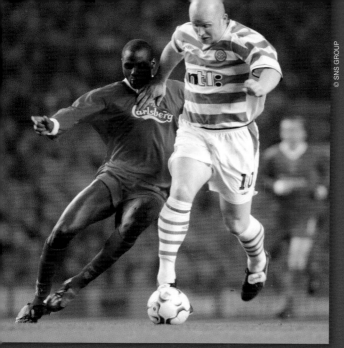

GOAL OF MY LIFE … scoring against Liverpool at Anfield in the UEFA Cup will live with me forever

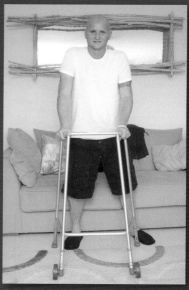

FIGHTING BACK … I lost six and a half stones in my battle with cancer, here's me on my zimmer after getting home. Hated that thing

HENKE AND HARTS … I loved playing with that man, 242 goals in 315 games for Celtic says it all

THE CELTIC DRAGON … celebrating one of my 14 goals for Wales, my 51 caps meant so much to me

I MISS YOU, MATE … the suicide of Gary Speed shattered everyone who was close to him, a class act as a man and a footballer

'ARRY'S GAME … Redknapp bought me for £3.2m at Hammers, I helped keep them up and he sold me to Wimbledon for £7.5m. Good business

IL CAPITANO … battling with Paolo Maldini against AC Milan. He was so good only his sons can wear that number 3 shirt now!

GORGEOUS GEORGE … gaffer Graham always looked the part and he knew his football too, I learned a lot at Arsenal

© SNS GROUP

© SNS GROUP

© SNS GROUP

THE WRIGHT STUFF ... Ian was an idol at Arsenal and taught me well, he even got to play in the Old Firm game like me

IN GORD I TRUST ... with Mark Wilson and Gordon Strachan at Celtic. He was a man I respected both as a coach and as a person

THERE'S ONLY ONE KEANO ... Roy might have lost on his debut at Clyde but he bossed an Old Firm game. Top-drawer

The greatest manager Celtic ever had put an off-the-cuff maverick winger into his master plan because he knew he would destroy defences without the shackles on him. That says it all. That's why with 130 goals in 515 games for Celtic, the one and only is my choice on the right. Jimmy Johnstone is in my Celtic Dream Team.

7

THE MIDDLE MAN

If I could have picked twelve men for this book then 'Ten-Thirty' would have been in the team. I wrestled long and hard with the central midfield selections and it is one that troubled me because I know enough of the stories, I have seen enough of the action, to know that Bertie Auld was some player. With Jinky Johnstone already in wide right in my first draft I couldn't see past his old pal Bertie at first, but I started to think whether the blend in midfield, something my old gaffer Martin O'Neill taught me about, was right and I had a rethink. So I hope Mr Auld will forgive me because I love playing golf with Bertie and he was a huge contender for a slot here because of that tenacious nature, the swagger and the character he brought to the Lisbon Lions.

The heart of midfield was a really difficult choice but you have to seriously think of Ten-Thirty in there. He remains immersed in the club and he loves the fans. I do a lot of Celtic functions with Bertie and what comes through is the desire he carried with him into every game the Lions played. He loved a tackle, and away from home he would go looking for the opposition's top player and he would nail him. The former Scotland boss Craig Brown called that ploy 'Kill the Chief'. I liked that! In Bertie's day it was simply a statement of intent in his eyes – Celtic were at your place and you weren't going to bully them. I see a bit of that in the current captain Scott Brown, who relishes that side of the game – especially at Ibrox!

My own Celtic team had a midfield that in my view was very carefully constructed by a manager not given enough credit for his tactical *nous*. Yes, we were big and strong and a huge threat at set-pieces and I remember talking to the former Kilmarnock coach Bobby Williamson about that aspect of facing us. Bobby was someone I admired and who thought deeply about the game and he told me his players were warned to within an inch of their lives about giving away cheap corners or needless free-kicks against us. We had myself, Mjallby, Balde, Varga, Sutton or Larsson all desperate to get on the end of headers and score. It scared him to death.

Yet there was a lot more to us than just that. Martin O'Neill looked at that 3-5-2 system we used and he put the right players in the right holes to make it work. One of those players was Neil Lennon, who faced Rangers captain Barry Ferguson at a time when they were both at their peak and I think those were great battles. Lenny took a lot of stick and I would always slaughter him saying he cost £5.75 million, which was way too much for someone who couldn't pass the ball forwards!

That was just my way of winding him up, though. I thought he was fantastic at breaking up the play and intercepting through balls, then he would get on it for us and he never gave it away. In that midfield three with him you would have Stiliyan Petrov who was always ready to chip in with a goal. In domestic football we would have Paul Lambert in there, and he was my favourite player to play with. Paul had this great appreciation of the game and he has carried that into management at Norwich City and now Aston Villa.

Lambo knew the job of the front man and he would roll the ball into you the right way then come and look for it back. And he was a great example of a player who educated himself and made himself so much better. The move to Borussia Dortmund literally changed his life. He learned so much under Ottmar Hitzfeld as they won the Champions League together in 1997 and he turned himself from a workaday attacking right-sided midfielder with Motherwell into the highly respected holding player in the best team in Europe that season. You just can't do that unless you have a sharp football brain.

Every time we took the field together I knew that I could trust Lambert to do the right thing, to find the right pass, because he recognised little moves the fans might not ever spot. He knew where I would run and he could deliver the telling ball. So often I would watch Stan Petrov bomb forward chasing a goal and there was Lambert slotting in ten yards behind him in the perfect position to cover. He did it selflessly time and again. Sit down with any player who knows the game and they will have recognised the craft he brought to that role. He played with his mind, not just his raw ability.

In Europe that system had Chris Sutton in that three instead of Lambert at times, which shows you the quality we had. On one side there would be the blistering pace of

Didier Agathe and on the other Alan Thompson, who had that wand of a left foot. Martin built that team on simplicity and that midfield fed a true superstar in Henrik Larsson. He scored 242 goals in 315 games for Celtic and earned the right to carry that mantle and it suited the rest of us to be the supporting cast.

Yet ask Henrik about Lambert and Lennon and you will hear instant respect because he knew how good they were at what they did. The same went for someone like Agathe, who could have been viewed as tactically naïve at times but had the steadying influence of the right-sided centre-half, Johan Mjallby, behind him. Johan would constantly be talking Didier through the game, telling him when to go and when to stay.

When I heard the news that Stan Petrov had been diagnosed with leukaemia, I was devastated. I couldn't believe that fate could be so cruel as to deal our closely knit team two massive body blows like that after my own battle with cancer. Yet I also knew that if anyone could beat that wretched disease it was Stan because he was the sort of boy who left every drop of sweat out on the training field in every training session. With that work ethic, though, came class as a footballer with a real eye for goal. That's invaluable in the modern game.

Again Stiliyan was a player who will always bless the day Martin O'Neill walked into Celtic because he had been bought in the John Barnes regime that turned sour on Celtic and was often used out of position at right-back. Stan was a lot of things but he wasn't a full-back. He was homesick for Bulgaria and I firmly believe that if Martin hadn't swept into power at the club we'd have lost one of the best players of the last decade.

Stan deserves to be mentioned in the same breath as the great players in this chapter and it's fitting that after the false start in the dark days of the Barnes regime that he got to work with the likes of Alan Thompson, Neil Lennon and Paul Lambert under Martin. Petrov was massive for us on the run to the UEFA Cup final in Seville, and I think the measure of him was that he flourished once the club provided him with quality around about him. In the end Stan gave seven years of superb service to Celtic and scored sixty-four goals in 311 matches.

Sometimes your time at a club comes to a natural end and after seven years in the Hoops I think in the cold light of day the fans will understand that Stan had to seek a new challenge, and that he would find it at Aston Villa under Martin, who trusted him so much. Celtic landed £6.5 million for a player who had cost just £2 million way back in 1999 and, as I've said before in this book, there are not too many times when the club can look at their transfer dealings in such a favourable light when it comes to recouping money. Whatever fans will think of the Dalglish–Barnes 'Dream Team' and everything that went wrong, the Petrov deal was a shrewd one.

If you ask the Hoops fans, I think they would tell you that the team Stan and I played in was the best Celtic side since the Lisbon Lions, and much of that came from the engine room Martin painstakingly pieced together.

As a striker I loved the plan of having a gifted player like Sutton in behind the front two, he was something else, Chris, but if I had to pick the best I played with in that position then it would have to be Dennis Bergkamp at Arsenal. I think everyone remembers that unbelievable spin turn that took him in to score a goal to die for at Newcastle United, but he did things like that every day in training. It didn't matter to him if there were 100,000 screaming fans there or three men and a dog, he just loved to show everyone the technique he had.

We called him 'The Iceman' at Highbury and for a period at the Gunners myself and Ian Wright played up front and we had Dennis playing just off us. I loved it – that was two years of footballing heaven. He wasn't as aggressive or competitive as Sutty was in that position. Dennis wouldn't track back and throw a tackle in, but he wreaked havoc in the final third. The likes of Tony Adams and Ian Wright consider Bergkamp to be a legend and I think that says it all. He is a genius and the best I ever played with in that position.

I have been lucky with the midfielders I have worked alongside in my career. I played with the great Roy Keane for six months at Celtic at the end of his playing days and I was in awe of him as a player. In training he treated every ball he gave away as a personal insult but he hardly tossed any away so he didn't have much reason to curse himself. He was just such a superb professional and his standards didn't drop one bit at Celtic.

I was never too sure how much of the Keane deal was down to the boss, Gordon Strachan, and how much was down to the board, who realised the lift it would give the place and the jerseys it would shift. This was a guy winding down his career but he was still one helluva player. It was the last hurrah for Roy and he had always said that as a boyhood Hoops supporter from County Cork, one of the last remaining ambitions he had left in football was to play for Celtic. As a fan he wanted to live that dream and for all that he had achieved this meant the world to him. He got off to a hellish start when we lost on his debut 2-1 in the Scottish Cup at Clyde, but that wasn't down to him. Graham Roberts, the ex-Rangers player, had them all fired up that day and we just didn't turn up. They deserved it on the day and we were desperately poor, we hardly made a chance.

I for one didn't turn around and blame Roy in the dressing room, or the Chinese centre-half Du Wei, who took a slaughtering in the press. I saw it simply as a collective nightmare. Clyde shocked us live on Sky, they were fantastic.

Last season I watched Kilmarnock win the CIS Cup against Celtic and that same dread began creeping into my bones as the game wore on. Killie's keeper Cammy Bell was having the game of his life and Lenny's boys just kept missing chances. I just had this awful feeling it was going to blow up in their faces and it did late on when Dieter van Turnhout scored the winner. They got turned over exactly the way we did at Clyde.

At first the Celtic dressing room had been quite surprised that Keane was coming in short-term in an area where we were quite well covered and we knew too that his hips were troubling him. So there were some misgivings amongst the senior professionals if I am honest, but he just blew them all away. His attitude was spot on. He made a lot of friends, he didn't make one single enemy that I can think of and he got on well with Neil Lennon, myself and the other big characters in that dressing room. He had ruled that United dressing room by fear and I knew that, but he hardly raised his voice at our place. Sure, if someone was sloppy in training and gave the ball away he would let them know about it, but that was a sign of what he demanded of himself and others and soon we would see that in the twilight of his career he still had what it takes on the big stage.

He still managed to totally boss the midfield when we won 1-0 at Ibrox in an Old Firm game and Majiec Zurawski scored the winner. I looked in wonder at him that day and also in his testimonial when Cristiano Ronaldo got the goal in front of 67,000 fans at Old Trafford and Keano played a half each for Celtic and United. He was peerless that night too.

We were all delighted to have the honour of playing in his testimonial and Roy made sure that every player from Celtic who was involved that night got a £2,000 Omega watch that I still wear with pride to this day. He was a consummate professional and my respect for the guy soared once I had played with him. I'm a great believer in the fact that it's not until you have shared a dressing room and a training pitch with a player that you begin to appreciate how good they really are. You can watch from the stands but you have to be there to see the glint in their eyes on an Old Firm day, as I did with Roy. He was my type of footballer and he was my type of person. There was so much hype around him that day against Rangers but he was the coolest man in Ibrox. It was as if he had played in a hundred Old Firm derbies.

We shouldn't have been surprised though. He had led the Republic of Ireland and captained Manchester United for the guts of a decade so he could handle even what that game would throw at him. He was up against Barry Ferguson, the Rangers captain who I rated as a player. In truth, I always felt that Rangers hung Barry out to dry over his V-sign controversy and his Boozegate blunder with Scotland. He was a silly boy then but I felt after the career he'd had the club could have stood up for him more. That day, though, he was fired up and at it, but Roy Keane made him look like a schoolboy. Roy ran the game from the centre of midfield and he was outstanding.

I know Roy's old team-mate Ronaldo takes some grief from some quarters but he has all the pace and the power in the world and he's got a cannon of a shot and that unique free-kick style in his armoury too. He is also terrific in the air and with a price tag of £80 million on the move from United to Real Madrid, I would have to put him down as one of the best I played against. I always thought it would be intriguing to see how he fared in Spain with Real Madrid because La Liga is to me the strongest league in the world. I have been to Real Sociedad, Barcelona, Valencia, Celta Vigo and the rest and I was always so impressed by the standard of their defenders.

So how do you come to terms with the Lionel Messi v Ronaldo goalscoring shootout last season when Messi scored seventy-two in the season and Ronaldo got sixty club goals? I mean, could they have scored that many in the English Premier League where Bergkamp prospered? That's a big debate because if the Spanish league is as strong as I used to think, then how can those guys score that heavily? Has it become a weaker championship because of the dominance of the Big Two? Are they just freaks of nature? It's only Manchester City or Chelsea who could afford Messi now, but one day I would love to see him come to British football to see if he could repeat that feat against the top Premiership defences.

The player I have chosen as the creative heartbeat of my Celtic Dream team may surprise some but I consider his to be a story of triumph through adversity. You see, if he had only thought of himself then Paul McStay wouldn't have stuck around to become a Celtic great. You look at Paul's career in Paradise and a little part of you wishes that he had been born twenty years later or ten years earlier. Then he could have been a part of the eras that saw Jock Stein and Martin O'Neill in charge of the Hoops.

Paul would have done a starting jersey justice with the Lisbon Lions or with my team that went all the way to the UEFA Cup final in Seville in 2003. Problem is he was born into an era when the club for long and painful stretches was stuck in the doldrums. Yet you can't live a football life based on regrets or what might have been. You have to examine the contribution McStay made in HIS time. And there is no question those were often testing days for the club he was born to play for. Truth is, when you look at those days, in particular the barren spell from the Scottish Cup win over Graeme Souness's Rangers in 1989 to Tommy Burns' triumph over Airdrie in the 1995 Cup final, then you will see Paul carrying the club on his back.

These days you can look at the lunacy of Liverpool paying out £35 million for Andy Carroll from Newcastle United and wonder what someone like McStay would have been worth if he had elected to pursue approaches from the likes of Inter Milan or Juventus and left Celtic. I know there was also cheeky interest at one time from Rangers boss Souness in Paul, but McStay doing a Mo Johnston and go and play for the other side? Do me a favour – not a chance.

Instead, as Celtic struggled, Paul continued to shine and his legend grew. That is some testament to him because he didn't have the chance to play alongside the Murdochs and the Aulds or even the Lamberts and the Lennons. As they grew up together in the Celtic team there was a real contrast between the flash, brash Charlie Nicholas and the humble quiet man McStay. Charlie, the Cannonball Kid, scored fifty-three goals in one season and had them all chasing him – Liverpool, Manchester United and Arsenal.

Nicholas chose the Gunners and looking back he might still regret that choice at the time. Was it a case of him choosing the bright lights of London over a purely foot-balling choice of Liverpool or United? Who knows, all I know is that his pal stuck around and they now sing his name in the Willie Maley song that has the line: 'They gave us James McGrory and Paul McStay'. That's some tribute.

If we are honest, he was the shining light of the Celtic teams he played for, and that's why I was always fasci-nated to be in his company when we lived close to each other in Houston in Renfrewshire. He was one of the first legends of Celtic I met and he went out of his way to come down with his wife Anne Marie and the kids to introduce himself as he knew I had two children of my own and we were trying to settle into a new area.

That gesture was typical of the man and Paul was great company, he was such a humble person and it upsets me that he is not a part of the club now, as he chose to move to Sydney in Australia and start a new life there. I don't know the story behind the scenes, maybe Celtic have given him a load of job offers and he just feels his time has passed there now, but for me, like Danny McGrain and the late Tommy Burns, he is the type of man who should always be in the fabric of the club.

McStay is so well respected by the Celtic family and it surprises me he is not involved. As a player I look upon Paul as a truly modern midfielder, in the same class as Steven Gerrard at Liverpool. He had a wonderful engine and had such great ability. He had a superb range of passing; he could bounce little one-twos off the striker or hit the killer raking ball to split a defence. He didn't shirk tackles and whilst I know his scoring ratio was always debated as too low I felt he was a real attacking threat and when he did score they were a bit special.

McStay had what I call 'game intelligence', much in the same way Paul Lambert had in my side. He knew when to hold his position and look at him when he scores a goal for Celtic and see the joy etched on his face. You can't fake that. His reaction shows how much it means to him and from the day he signed on February 20, 1981 until the ankle injury that forced him to retire early in 1997 Paul was a one-club man. He is someone as woven into the history of Celtic as Gerrard is at Liverpool. You can't picture them playing in another jersey.

He is like McNeill in the '60s and '70s – he summed up what the club stood for and he lived with the pressure right from the day he scored a couple of goals for Scotland as a fifteen-year-old kid in the 5-4 schoolboys win over England in 1980. From that day forward he was marked out as special but he coped with all the hype and was always such a grounded person. His great uncles Jimmy and Willie were legends at the club and that family history carries some responsibility with it. You see some players crash and burn with that kind of heat on them but in my eyes Paul thrived on it, and he became a true Celtic great. The best players blank out all that white noise around them, they are driven to be the best they can be.

In his time at Celtic Paul won three titles, four Scottish Cups and a League Cup. The championships were days to cherish, he was inspirational in the unforgettable 1986 triumph as the Hoops humbled St Mirren 5-0 and Dundee's Albert Kidd scored twice to break Hearts in a dramatic final-day finish.

McStay's true season in the sun, though, came in the club's centenary year of 1988 when he was voted Scotland's Player of the Year and he was a pivotal presence in the team that won the Double under Billy McNeill. The club and the Celtic board's failure to build on that success must anger Paul even now. McStay played through an era when there was a damning lack of investment in the players around him. He played through all the boardroom unrest and he kept his dignity and he kept playing for the Hoops. That was the measure of the man.

To play for the club you love is a very powerful thing, I suppose I will always carry a little regret in my heart that I didn't get the chance to play for Swansea City, who remain my first love in this game. These days I have a seat in my box at the Liberty Stadium and I can go to watch Michael Laudrup's side against the best the Premiership has to offer.

Back in the day I would stand on the North Bank at the Vetch and watch the Swans languishing in the bottom rung of the English game in front of 4,000 fans. It was a question of timing, I didn't sign for them as a kid and then I developed quickly and was soon a £2 million teenager at Arsenal when I signed from Luton Town.

So when I was a prized asset in the Premiership with the likes of Arsenal, West Ham and Wimbledon, my home-town team were still struggling and trying to make their way through the leagues and it just wasn't feasible for me to go there.

I did have a little chance of going there when I was at West Brom and Tony Mowbray put me out on loan at Norwich City, but the Swans boss Roberto Martinez didn't want the deal and it didn't happen. I hold no grudges there, I thought Roberto was a great manager who brought such an invigorating passing style to my club and if I am honest my own fires were fading a little by then. So, yes, it gnaws at me a little that I can't say John Hartson once of Swansea City but I have too much to be thankful for in my football career to dwell on that one negative.

With Paul I think deep down he never wanted want to leave Celtic. Everyone remembers the day he threw his jersey into The Jungle in 1992 and that looked like the grand farewell gesture. I have no doubts that at that point Paul had made his mind up that this was the summer he would go. Yet something kept tugging at him, this special club kept pulling him back and for the next five years he dedicated himself to the Hoops again. He was happy in Glasgow, his family mean the world to him, they were settled and he was not a man driven by money. So he stayed put and I understand that completely because he was never out of the team, it was always built around him and all of his emotions were tied up in the place. That's a compelling mix. Yet it was one that kept him at a club who couldn't provide him with the standard of team-mates he deserved and it was heartbreaking that in 1994 when the League Cup final against little Raith Rovers came around it should be Paul who was the scapegoat for a humiliating defeat. The game was tied 2-2 after extra-time at Ibrox and it went to the lottery of the penalty shootout. Sudden death came and McStay missed and the critics had their field day questioning his bottle.

Courage? He had stayed around to captain one of the poorest Celtic sides in recent memory and he stayed because of his love for the club. I missed a League Cup final penalty the day we lost against Rangers so I know how he felt that awful day. It is gutting and it haunts you as a footballer. Yet six months later he was skipper as TB's team beat Airdrie to lift the Scottish Cup, and I think his quote from that day sums up a lot of the anguish he went through serving Celtic as the archetypal one-club man. He said, 'That game was ninety minutes on paper but for me it lasted as long as my five years as skipper or the six years we have spent without a trophy.'

Great players leave legacies and Paul McStay did one of the famous Celtic family proud. In 1985 they got to look on as Paul and his brother Willie, now such a distinguished coach, emulated their great uncles Jimmy and Willie and won the Scottish Cup together.

Paul can come back from his new life in Oz and show his kids his picture in the Scottish Football Hall of Fame. He was skipper when the Under-18s won the European Championship in 1982, the only major trophy the country has won. He was the only player to play for Scotland at youth, Under-21 and full international level in the space of a calendar year. I mean, take a breath and think about that one. Some feat eh?

Paul went on to win seventy-six caps for Scotland, scoring nine goals, and he sparkled at Euro 92 when he battered in a trademark shot against the Commonwealth of Independent States in the closing 3-0 win that followed narrow defeats from Holland and Germany. It was after those finals that the rumours of a move to Inter Milan intensified, but just as talk of a switch to Seville and Spurs had petered out earlier in his career, the prospect of a move to Serie A ebbed away. Who knows if he would have taken it – there's something in me that says Paul couldn't have brought himself to quit Celtic if it had come down to it. Some players are just made to play in green and white.

Paul McStay is called 'The Maestro' by the fans and those tags tell a story, whether it is Henrik Larsson the King of Kings, or Big Bad John Hartson. The supporters bestow those nicknames upon players for a reason. He pulled all the strings in the teams he played for, and that's why he just edged out Bertie Auld for me in the heart of the midfield. Paul has to be in there because of the loyalty, the devotion and the skill he showed in a whole career spent at Paradise.

That's why Paul McStay is in my Celtic Dream Team.

8

THE ENGINE ROOM

You know you are special when you have left Celtic and then, when you come back to play on the hallowed turf, the fans chant for you to sign for the club again. That seldom happens for players who choose to walk away from the honour of wearing the Hoops, but it happened for Davie Hay. After seven years at the club and 230 games Davie had departed for Chelsea in 1974 and left the fans who idolised him dejected.

The first season after his departure the ten-in-a-row dream died and many of the punters even now put that down to the Celtic board allowing Davie to be lured south in an era when they were unwilling to lay out the money required to keep their best talents. Still, there is always that feeling of deep disappointment in the hearts of some fans who will blame the player for taking the better contract because they can't understand why he would ever leave Celtic. That's what makes the reaction to Hay's return to Paradise in May 1976 stick in my mind. It's the sort of emotion that makes the club special.

Davie was back at Celtic Park to play for us as a guest in the star-studded Jimmy Johnstone/Bobby Lennox testimonial game against Manchester United. Kenny Dalglish, himself just a year away from a departure south to Liverpool, scored a hat-trick that night in a 4-0 win, but it was Davie who ran the show and the fans chanted, 'We Want Hay'. That emotional reaction to seeing Davie in the side again prompted rumours he might return but it never happened, which is a shame.

Davie is one of those great football men to be in the company of, he knows the game inside-out and he was bred as a Celtic player in one helluva environment. He was part of the Quality Street Gang – the Celtic reserves of the late '60s that also included Dalglish, Danny McGrain and George Connelly.

Hay was a right-back at first but I think I am justified in pondering him for my Dream Team in midfield because I feel he was a real driving force from that position in all I have read or seen of him as a Celtic player. Jock Stein recognised the ball-winning qualities Davie had in his locker and even trusted him to play at left-back in the 1969 League Cup final win over St Johnstone after the big man kicked Tommy Gemmell out of the team following another one of their bust-ups. When you read the history it seems like Tommy had the knack of pressing the big man's buttons! Anyhow, with Tam out, Bertie Auld scored the winner and Hay was off and running as a big-time Celtic star.

It's a sign of Davie's class and versatility that he shone at right-back in the 1970 European Cup semi-final win against Leeds United and was excellent in the final defeat from Feyenoord too when other players, by their own frank admission afterwards, simply didn't perform when it mattered most. Right-back, left-back, midfield and even at times filling in at centre-half, Hay was a complete player and I know many fans who think the fact that Davie was out injured in the European Cup semi-final against Inter Milan in 1972 was a key factor in the Hoops eventually sliding to defeat on penalties.

By the time Davie was a pivotal reason for the title triumph in 1973, he was an established Scotland star who felt he knew his worth and, alongside his great pal George Connelly, he lurched into a bitter dispute with the club over wages. That's a theme that runs through so many stories of players in Celtic's past and I think, while there always has to be a balance struck, that it has been to the club's lasting benefit that in my heyday Martin O'Neill dragged the club into the modern era in terms of what is needed to put a successful side out on the park.

Back then, though, Davie was fighting a war with the boardroom yet eventually when a fragile peace was brokered he returned to the team and he just did what he always did and excelled in every position he played in. Davie went to the World Cup finals in West Germany in 1974 with Scotland knowing, I'm sure, that he was in the shop window. That's certainly how it worked out, as the man they called 'The Quiet Assassin' was brilliant in a side that came home from the finals undefeated. Alright, it was the same old Scottish story of glorious failure, a 2-0 win over Zaire, a 1-1 draw with Yugoslavia then an agonising 0-0 draw with Brazil. Hay, though, walked away with his head held high as he went into battle alongside Billy Bremner and won their midfield tussle against the legendary Brazilian Roberto Rivelino and his sidekicks. Davie then came home and found Chelsea, Spurs and Manchester United were chasing him. It makes me shake my head in bewilderment now when I hear he would have stayed for another £10 a week. Instead, the club took the £225,000 bid from Chelsea and sold off a huge part of the future of the team. Those sort of decisions come back to haunt football clubs but Davie's love for Celtic meant he returned as manager in the 1980s and he remains a part of the fabric of the place to this day.

When I considered my choices for roles in the engine room of this Dream Team, Davie had to be there and so did his buddy George Connelly, a player who still carries such mystique around Celtic Park. I know little about the problems that haunted George's Hoops career and I won't recount them in great detail here – all I know is that every true Celtic supporter I know who was around in that era talks of the big fella in almost reverential tones. They just loved him and they mourn for what he could have been.

He achieved enough as it was. Jock Stein had sent him out to entertain the fans with some keepie-uppie at a Euro tie when he was a kid and the place was in raptures. All the Lions boys tell me big George regularly did 2,000 touches for a warm-up! You look at those guys from that Quality Street Gang reserve team – Dalglish, McGrain, Hay, Macari, Connelly. Wow. What a sight they must have been for other teams when they were playing together in the stiffs, it must have been a nightmare. Imagine you are some poor guy from Dunfermline coming back from an injury and looking to get a quiet ninety minutes in the reserves under your belt and then that lot run out.

Again, like Hay, Connelly showed he could square up to the best in that European Cup semi-final win over Leeds and I know from my own clashes with the likes of Blackburn Rovers and Liverpool in our run to Seville how much playing the English gets your back up. Don't kid yourself that you Scots have a monopoly on the love of beating them! I'm Welsh, for God's sake!

George was Player of the Year in 1973 and he had the world at his feet but maybe as a quiet guy from Fife that was the problem right there. His marriage failed and George had troubles with drink and it is all just terribly sad. I have been through a divorce in the goldfish bowl of Glasgow as a footballer myself. It's hellish. I'm not blaming anyone else, I'm just trying to give you a little insight into how someone like George might have felt then. I caused my break-up, I had an affair. It was no fling though, as my wife Sarah and I are now so happy with our two little girls Lina and Stephanie-Kari who have added to the joy of my daughter Rebecca and my son Joni from my first marriage. Yet I know how much hurt it all caused. The fact is that my divorce finished me at Celtic and in the end it finished me as a footballer, so I know what it is like to have troubles that drag you down despite all the adulation you get as a Celtic player.

Those pressures plagued George. He walked out on Scotland as they were getting on a plane for international duty and Billy McNeill told me he once completed a gruelling pre-season run on a course called Cardiac Hill then kept on going to his car and disappeared for days. I understand fans reading stories like George Connelly's and asking themselves how a player could get to the stage where they feel the world is crowding in on them. Again,

I have lived inside that world, and where George's vice may have been his drinking, mine was gambling. There were times when I did my *Audience with John Hartson* shows that I couldn't bring myself to talk about the gambling that gripped me when I was at the peak of my powers. I was ashamed and embarrassed by the person I became when all I cared about at times was my next visit to the bookies.

I was betting on American football and sports I knew nothing about. Throwing away fortunes until Sarah gave me the ultimatum and sorted me out. Now we go together to Gamblers Anonymous, we sit at the meetings and I share the pain I've gone through. I have learned that like the drink, gambling is an addiction. I'm clean now and I feel proud of that in a way, but I know I will always be a gambler and that I have to fight it day by day. My addiction has brought me so much stress. Look, footballers are just people. I wore green and white the same way George Connelly did, but we carried all of our frailties inside it.

It's sad that I'm told now that when Davie Hay went to Chelsea, George's heart went out of it and, again, I recognise the pain that causes as, at thirty-three, when I decided to hang up my boots, my fires had gone out and for a time I didn't love the game the same way I do once again now or as I did as a kid growing up.

There will always be a world of regrets around a man like George Connelly who calls himself a 'wasted talent' and what he turned his back on the day he walked out on Celtic. Yet perhaps now we should celebrate what he gave when he did play. The likes of big Jock compared him to Franz Beckenbauer and marvelled at his technical ability, and that is more than enough to put him in contention in this chapter.

When you talk football with Billy McNeill, as I often do at social gatherings these days, it's understandable that you get around to debating the players he signed when he was Celtic manager. There were few better than Murdo MacLeod. Billy reckons that although the £100,000 he paid to Dumbarton was looked upon as a fortune at the time, he got a bargain the day he landed Murdo. I played in so many great games for Celtic that it would be churlish to use the word jealous about the occasions another player savoured. I've got to admit, though, it would have been something special to play the night Ten Men Won the League against Rangers on May 21, 1979. And can you imagine the feeling if you were Murdo, smashing home the clincher with a twenty-five-yard rocket to seal it at 4-2? Murdo was an all-action midfielder, a real powerhouse, and again when you examine his record you can see he had some of his greatest nights in Europe at our place. He scored memorable goals against the likes of Juventus and I think those are the sorts of occasions when you prove yourself as a Celtic player.

With Paul McStay already selected, you could put a solid case for Murdo to play by his side because the evidence is already there. In 1983 – when Celtic succumbed to Dundee United in the title race – Murdo finished the season with nineteen goals from the heart of midfield. That shows you the punch he packed from there and whether it was left-back or in a more defensive role in midfield when McStay began to flourish, managers like McNeill and Hay could always bank on MacLeod.

Murdo was one of the few Scots who had the wisdom and courage to take his move abroad at the right time in 1987. The £250,000 fee from Borussia Dortmund meant that after nine great seasons in the Hoops big Billy's initial £100,000 outlay did indeed look like a steal. Then, when Murdo's new team drew Celtic in the UEFA Cup in his first season in exile, the warmth he was shown by the Celtic fans despite their team going out 3-2 on aggregate showed his place in the fans' hearts was secure. That was further cemented when Murdo returned to the club as Wim Jansen's number 2 and helped derail Rangers' nine-in-a-row bid in 1998. It's a pity that Wim's rows with general manager Jock Brown meant his reign lasted only one season and Murdo followed the Dutch coach out the door. These days he earns his corn partly as a media pundit and has a column in the *Daily Record* giving his insight on the game. He has earned the right, that's for sure.

Murdo always played with his heart on his sleeve for Celtic and another cast from the same mould would be Peter Grant, who had such a deep love for the Hoops. Like his close friend Paul McStay, he had the club running through his veins. I loved his attitude and what he brought to Celtic. He didn't have the ability of a Lambert or a Petrov, but one Celtic manager after another placed their trust in him and that says so much. He gave every shred of himself to the cause in every game he played for the club. Burns and Grant were men who suffered with the club they loved through their toils and savoured their successes, and I couldn't have written this book without mentioning either of them.

The best I played with in the heart of midfield set me thinking back to the Arsenal days and the joy of sharing a pitch with the likes of the Swede Stefan Schwarz and John Jensen, who were both committed and technical mid-fielders. Jensen won the European Championships with Denmark in 1992 and he was always a player I felt was hugely under-rated. None of them, though, could top Roy Keane, for the reasons I have mentioned in the previous chapter, and he goes into the Best I Played With XI, thanks to those six months we spent together in the Hoops.

Played against? No question about this one – it has to be Bryan Robson, the captain of Manchester United and England and one of the most fearsome competitors I ever came up against. Robbo was injured so often in my eyes for one reason only: because he was so incredibly brave. Call me cynical if you like but I look at these players who play 250 consecutive games with more than a hint of suspicion. I think that sort of record means that you are not committing to challenges and you are not getting hurt. Robson was dislocating his shoulder or injuring his knee hurling himself in there to win balls for his team. I reckon that I played with injuries perhaps 75 to 80 per cent of my career. Otherwise I would never have played, and I saw so many players throughout my career who I felt were psychologically bottling it because of a fear of injury. Me? I say strap yourself up and get on with it, I very seldom played without a niggle of some sort.

Robson missed a lot of big games because of that sort of commitment but I would have loved to have had him in the trenches beside me. I played against him when he was at the end of his career for Middlesbrough and he played at centre-half one night at Highbury. He was thirty-nine and I was twenty-one at Arsenal but I never got a kick that night and the man just frustrated the hell out of me because I just could not get a hold of the ball. He knew physically he couldn't fight me for possession, I was twice the size of him. Instead he just out-thought me, and he kept leaning on me, nudging me, getting his toe in front of me to nick it away. I was going mental and I eventually got sent off for shouting and swearing at the referee! Robbo drove me nuts that night, but he was some player.

This was a slot in my side that brought so many players into my thoughts: Bertie Auld, Davie Hay, George Connelly, Murdo MacLeod – there are so many great names to consider. Yet when it came to the man to partner Paul McStay at the heart of my team my mind went back to the start for me at Celtic. I arrived in Glasgow in the wake of the death of the great Bobby Murdoch. He had suffered a stroke and was taken from us at the age of just fifty-six. I remember the real sense of shock there was amongst his friends in the Lions team. He was the first one of them to die and they were all just distraught, this band of brothers who made history as the first British team to lift the European Cup.

During my time at Celtic I met Jim Craig, Tommy Gemmell, John Clark, Billy McNeill, Jimmy Johnstone, Bertie Auld, Bobby Lennox and Stevie Chalmers. Even Joe McBride – who we lost earlier this year – had stopped me to have a kind word about what life was like as a Celtic striker. I'd met so many men from that legendary team but I hadn't met Bobby Murdoch, and that will always be a regret because I came to learn just how much he meant to that team of legends. Almost every Lion I would talk to – even Jimmy Johnstone, who was voted the Greatest Ever Celt – would tell me that Bobby Murdoch was the best player in that team. He must have been something else. He made his first-team debut for Celtic as a seven-teen-year-old kid against Hearts in a 3-1 win, getting the nod because his team-mate, John Divers, had forgotten his boots!

Can you imagine that one being explained away when they do the team news on Sky Soccer Saturday? Jeff Stelling turning to Merson and saying, 'Well, Paul, Divers is out of the Celtic line-up. The reason? He's only gone and forgotten his boots!' That would be priceless. Seriously, though, this one in truth was a difficult choice for me to make because I haven't seen so much of Bobby Murdoch in action but I know from talking to his old team-mates that that is my loss. Their evidence, what they said to me about Bobby, means he MUST be in there. Simple as that.

There was a lot of research that went into this book – looking at autobiographies, hitting the internet sites – which was something I had done during my Celtic career, as I've said. The history of the club is fascinating and means a lot to me, and whilst Bobby was a quiet man, what others said about him speaks volumes:

'As far as I am concerned, Bobby Murdoch is just about the best player I had as manager.'

– Jock Stein

'Bobby Murdoch is my complete footballer.'

– Helenio Herrera, Inter Milan manager

Those two quotes are just for starters, the more I read the more Bobby's story drew me in. They talk about players missing the boat in terms of earnings. Well, how much would Bobby Murdoch be worth in the market if he were playing today? The older generation of fans I have spoken to just adored him and he was at the core of a very special team. He was also a man of the people, signing for Celtic in 1959 when he was on £3 a week as a sheet-metal worker. Bobby knew the kind of graft that was waiting for him if he didn't make it with a ball at his feet.

I was looking for a blend in this midfield and once I decided Paul McStay had to be in there then it was a toss-up between Bobby and his Lions team-mate Bertie Auld and the nod went Murdoch's way. I am so proud of being part of a very exclusive club, the group of men who have scored 100 goals for Celtic, that I have that tattoo with my 110 total etched on my right arm. Bobby Murdoch had a ratio of 105 in 484 games for Celtic, and that's from midfield. If he was playing in the modern game he would be the equivalent of Chelsea's Frank Lampard or Liverpool skipper Steven Gerrard. Stiliyan Petrov gave my team that goalscoring menace and Murdoch could have done that for my Dream Team, the perfect foil for McStay.

To get that sort of total from a deeper role is just phenomenal and eleven of those goals came in his fifty-seven European ties, which shows he could produce on the big stage too. Paul McStay perhaps didn't score as many as he should have but this fella would more than make up for that. Again you have to look at the genius of big Jock for rescuing Bobby's career. He was planning to emigrate to Australia because he was really toiling at Celtic and down in the dumps about how his career was going, but then Mr Stein arrived and tweaked his position from inside-right to right-half.

When you read the stories of the Lions, that would happen time and again. Stevie Chalmers, who would write his name in football history with that poacher's reaction to turn home Murdoch's shot in the European Cup final against Inter Milan, was a right-winger when Stein arrived in Paradise. Big Jock looked at him and thought there was something else there, though, and he was changed to play through the middle. It was a masterstroke – and it was the same for Bobby. That one little switch was the catalyst for Murdoch's rise at the club and he drove forward from that and into the history books. It reminds me of Martin O'Neill paying £50,000 to Hibs to sign Didier Agathe. He knew he couldn't play him as an out-and-out orthodox right-back but as a wing-back it was a different kettle of fish. He was made for it. Next thing you know Didier is being rated at £5 million and huge clubs throughout Europe are looking at him.

Throughout his days in the Hoops Murdoch averaged around ten goals a season from midfield, most of them from Bertie Auld cutbacks, if you believe what Bertie keeps telling me! Seriously, Bertie still raves about one performance from Bobby in the 1972 Scottish Cup final against Hibernian. Murdoch was the architect of a 6-1 destruction of the Hibees that day, and although Paulo Sergio's Hearts came close to murdering the green and white side of Edinburgh by the same scoreline in 2012, they came up one short. That's still a record hammering in a final, and Bobby was the man whose name was written all over that historic game.

I was lucky enough to meet Bobby's lovely wife Kathleen in a Glasgow restaurant not long after his death, and she was so complimentary about my move and how I was doing at the club. It shone through how much her husband meant to her and my heart went out to her.

You know, there's this great story of big Jock sending Bobby to a health farm in England to lose weight because he always struggled with that. The manager said Murdoch came back heavier, with a load of bad betting tips from all the racing jockeys he'd met in there! I have sympathy with that. I always struggled with my size and I remember one summer Harry Redknapp at West Ham said I had returned for pre-season training 33lbs overweight. To be fair, I was quite happy with that – I thought it was 40lbs! So I know the jibes that Bobby will have faced; I had them thrown at me my whole career. My answer was always to say just have a look at the managers who signed me and the fees they paid for me. If you're overweight and unfit, you don't score nine Old Firm goals – and remember it should have been eleven because two were disallowed for nothing!

At my peak at Celtic I was a lean, mean fighting machine. Harry bought me for £3.2 million then sold me to Wimbledon for £7.5 million after I had scored the goals to keep West Ham in the Premier League. Harry did all right out of me. So, weight? Look at Paul Gascoigne, who played the best football of his career in eighteen memorable months at Rangers when he was half a stone overweight and he could get his arm across people and keep them off the ball. Kenny Dalglish used to stick that big backside of his out and defenders couldn't get near him.

So if Murdoch was a little over what he could have been and looking a little heavy in his Celtic shorts, well, so what? I was never going to look like Larsson or Sutton in my kit. That was the way my frame was but it made managers pay £20 million for me in transfer fees throughout my career. Martin O'Neill, Joe Kinnear and Harry Redknapp don't buy duds – they buy top players. So in all seriousness, forget the weight issue that is often dragged up around Murdoch. In my eyes, when you listen to what Jock Stein said about Bobby then you can see that it's all just a myth.

Bobby Murdoch won nineteen top honours in fourteen magnificent years at Celtic. Eight titles, five Scottish Cups, five League Cups and, of course, the European Cup. He was the football writers' Player of the Year in 1969. So for all those who want to point to the fact he might have carried some extra timber, I'd say he was worth his weight in trophies. Murdoch moved on to Jack Charlton's Middlesbrough when he left Celtic and played a key role in mentoring a young midfielder there called Graeme Souness. When he was asked about that as Souness's Ibrox Revolution swung into action in 1986, Bobby grimaced. 'I wish I hadn't bothered.' Souness, though, has always insisted one of the Lisbon Lions' favourite sons played a major role in the making of him as a footballer. I consider Graeme to have been one of the great British midfielders and it's clear he felt Murdoch was a voice always worth listening to.

Graeme stressed, 'He came along at just the right time, not just for me but for the whole team. His experience settled us as we went for promotion and got it, he was such a big influence on my career. Bobby was such an excellent passer of the ball and he would always pull me to one side and tell me if he thought that I was acting wrongly.' It is testimony to what Murdoch brought to the Teesside club that he is fondly remembered even now for his part in the promotion campaign and what he gave to Boro in 125 games in the red and white.

Bobby had an ill-fated spell as manager there but the fans refuse to hold it against him, instead he is held in high esteem for what he gave them as a midfield schemer and for nurturing talents like Souness in the winter of his career with his boots on. You don't get the nickname 'Chopper' if you don't like a tackle, right enough, and there is one brilliant picture in the archives you see of Bobby confronting Sir Alex Ferguson in his days as a Rangers striker and growling ferociously at him in the midst of one of those mad Old Firm games. Funnily enough, Fergie never played for Gers again!

Murdoch's total of just twelve caps for Scotland is a puzzling one that will always have the Celtic fans looking at conspiracy theories, especially when you see that he scored six goals for his country in those matches in the '60s. All I can think of to explain that is that Scotland did have an embarrassment of riches in midfield at the time. Closer investigation of his international record shows that he played against England in 1966 at Hampden when he was ill and again three years later when the entire Scottish side flopped and were hammered 4-1. Perhaps those setbacks were never forgiven.

It seems a paltry cap haul, though, for a man of Bobby's proven ability and even a memorable goal against West Germany in a qualifier for Mexico 70 wasn't enough. Scotland didn't make it and the World Cup stage was denied the Murdoch talents, which is a crying shame.

In later life Bobby walked with a stick and was haunted by pain from an ankle problem that had plagued his career and he won a historic case to get compensation from the state when it was treated as an industrial injury. He carried a heavy toll with him from his playing career for the rest of his days.

You just have to look at those words of the two gaffers in the 1967 European Cup final to know what a significant player Bobby Murdoch was. Herrera called him the complete footballer and Stein said he was one of the best he had ever bossed. If I didn't have Billy McNeill in my side then those words would have been enough to make sure this man was my captain. That's high praise and that's why Bobby Murdoch is in my Celtic Dream Team.

9

THE WIDE BHOYS

'Thank you for the kind messages big man, TB'.

That was the heartrending text left on my phone just a week before we lost one of the greatest Celtic men who ever lived. Tommy Burns. I never realised how serious his skin cancer was and it really hit me like a hammer that he could be taken away at the age of just fifty-one. That happened before my own battle with cancer which I tackle elsewhere in this book and it just left me feeling empty and bereft. Jimmy Johnstone was the Greatest Ever Celt, followed closely by Henrik Larsson for me, but if you were to pick a man who embodied every single thing that is good about Celtic, I'm sure they would both have said it all lived in one man – Tommy Burns.

TB was just a wonderful Celtic man and he was revered by the supporters, who I think took him to their hearts because they realised his love for their club was deep and genuine. There was no hollow badge-kissing or chest-thumping, nothing false about him, he was a true gentleman.

I don't think anyone can forget those images of the current Rangers manager Ally McCoist and Gers legend

Walter Smith carrying the coffin of their friend, who they had worked with in the Scotland set-up. Ally's face just crumpled in grief as he burst into floods of tears and it showed you how much TB meant to them. And amidst all the emotion and the sadness we feel that Tommy was taken from us so young, I think we should always remember what a good player he was. Tommy twists, Tommy turns, Tommy Burns.

There's something about left-footed players that makes them look more elegant on the ball. My nephew James who has won a contract at Portsmouth is all left peg and he looks great the minute he takes possession. Unlike his Uncle John did at times! I think it was that way with Tommy when you saw him bursting forward from mid-field and going at the opposition. With a lot of those creative types, though, they didn't fancy the dirty work, the tracking back and the closing down. You couldn't say that about TB, though, he gave every ounce he had every time he played for Celtic.

Tommy was just twenty when he first felt the burden of the weight of responsibility thrust upon his shoulders following Kenny Dalglish's £440,000 departure to my boyhood heroes Liverpool. The following season Celtic were still hurting and they hurtled down to fifth in the league and missed out on Europe. In times like that big clubs need someone to cling onto, the fans need someone to relate to, and TB took the heat, along with the likes of Roy Aitken, and he suffered until Billy McNeill took over and the cavalry arrived in the shape of Davie Provan and Murdo MacLeod.

Still, though, they'll tell you that Tommy wrestled with controlling his temper when things went against him and when we were all together at Celtic I remember Gordon Strachan recalling that TB was sent off at Pittodrie for scything into him during a heated clash with Aberdeen. To be fair, even Tommy confessed he deserved a red card for that one – it must be something with these gingers. Lenny is the same. It has never affected me, as I am strawberry blond! Seriously, at various times when you look back at his career Tommy Burns was linked with Arsenal and then the likes of Chelsea and Everton but always there would be something pulling him back to the club he loved.

Tommy went through so much as a player at Celtic before he even returned to take on the mantle of manager that it was fitting that he should leave the club the right way after he'd been offered a role as player-coach at Kilmarnock in December 1989. He said goodbye to the Celtic fans after a friendly clash against Ajax and when he was subbed in the second half he ran to The Jungle to throw his boots to the fans. There wasn't a dry eye in the house, but no-one could know that just nineteen years later we would be mourning him for real. I still miss Tommy today but in quieter moments I just think positively and remember how privileged I am to have known him, to have shared a training pitch and a barrowload of laughs with him.

If Tommy Burns is a contender to fill the slot on the left of midfield then we also have to look at the credentials of John Collins. Paul McStay and John were the shining lights in some dark days for Celtic and it should be remembered that Collins could have taken the easy way out when his performances for Hibs meant that he was valued at £1 million and he was having big-money moves dangled in front of him. Graeme Souness and Rangers wanted him, the carrot was there, but he turned his nose up at it and played for the club I know he loves and will always support deep down. I have had the pleasure of working with John on TV with the likes of ESPN and he is an education to listen to. He was a terrific player and he had what I call a pillow touch on that left foot – imagine yourself throwing a tennis ball with all your might at a pillow. It drops dead and John can do that with a football battered at him at pace because he has what I call a 'soft' left foot. Just such a deft touch.

I don't think any Celtic fan should begrudge John the eventual Bosman move he made to Monaco because for the six years he spent in the Hoops he only had a solitary Scottish Cup win to show for it and he had laboured away with only really Tom Boyd and Paul McStay, who were in the same class as him. He knew he could learn in French football and, in fact, the move there changed his life in so many ways. He loved the lifestyle off the park and the diet, preparation and sheer professionalism on it was a real eye-opener for him. I love to sit and listen to John talk about football because he is very knowledgeable about what makes top players tick. He is passionate about seeing the game played the right way. Even now John is in magnificent shape and I know his Hibs players were envious of his six-pack before he lost his job at Easter Road and he's forty-four years of age now!

Collins was one of the first players to wear those Adidas Predator boots and swerved a couple of great goals in against Rangers with them and I know, like me, that he relished the experience of doing that! And I think he showed why he should be on this list in the English

Premiership too. He played with my Welsh international boss, Chris Coleman, at Fulham – he was a great admirer of John's and of the professionalism he brought to Craven Cottage. The Everton fans loved him when Walter Smith took John there too and I remember him bossing a game against us when I was at West Ham, and he was superb.

Doing this book has made me think deeply about one aspect of my time in Glasgow in particular – that I was a lucky boy to be at Celtic in such a successful period. You look at players like Boyd, McStay and Collins and what they went through in tougher eras for the club and I realise that now. Out of the five titles I contested for Celtic we won three and I lost two on the final day. Of those last-day losses one was by one goal when Rangers beat Dunfermline 6-1 in the last game to clinch it and the other came when Scott McDonald scored twice in the dying minutes to rip it away from us at Motherwell. Both those days still haunt me, but at least I was in the hunt. A great player like John Collins didn't get a title medal with Celtic and that puts my hard times into perspective.

Also in the shake-up for the jersey on the left of midfield is a player so good that Jock Stein signed him TWICE, Tommy Callaghan. Stein signed Callaghan for Dunfermline and returned to bring him to Paradise, and they say he suffered at first from an inferiority complex because he was operating alongside the likes of Bobby Murdoch and Bertie Auld. In some ways, who could blame him? These guys were the legends and Tommy was the new Bhoy in town and until the 1969 League Cup final against St Johnstone when he sparkled and Auld got the winner, he struggled. That day was a turning point for him. When you study the Callaghan career you can see the influence he grew to have on Celtic in the second half of the nine-in-a-row run. At the start of the 1971-72 season he played a major role in three wins at Ibrox in four mad weeks and scored a belter in one 3-0 win over Rangers. That must have been a good month to be a Gers fan!

Tommy wasn't noted for crunching tackles, he preferred to run from deep and start moves and some fans wanted more blood and snotters from him, but there is no question this was a class act as a footballer. When he finally departed for Clydebank in 1976 in a £10,000 move, he left with six league winner's medals, three Scottish Cups and two League Cups. Not bad for someone who started out thinking he wasn't good enough for Celtic.

So there were options for me to mull over wide-left in this Heaven's Eleven and this chapter brought back a lot of memories of a very special man. If I'd had a substitutes' bench for this wonderful Dream Team of mine then Tommy Burns would have been fighting for a place on it alongside the likes of Brian McClair and Paolo di Canio. They all played the game the Glasgow Celtic way. Rest in peace, TB.

Yes, you could make a case for the likes of Burns, Callaghan or Collins to get the nod here and I'm sure there are others the fans could debate. Me? I had this role pegged out for one man when I sat down with my Dream Team and knew I had to settle on a certain pairing up front. It meant adapting the job out left, it meant finding a way to get Bobby Lennox into the team. And I don't think it's a stretch to play Bobby here; in fact, he's made for it. Lennox's scoring record of 273 goals in 571 Celtic games puts him second only to Jimmy McGrory – the manager who signed him for the club – in the all-time list and above the great Henrik Larsson, who lies third. So in constructing my Celtic Dream team, there simply had to be a place for Bobby Lennox.

Bobby's record in finding the back of the net is phenomenal and that is all the more remarkable because he played a lot of his games out wide. We were together at the opener for this 2012-13 season when Celtic won 1-0 against Aberdeen in August and we had been asked to help carry round the flag to celebrate 125 years of the Hoops. I told Bobby then that I had put him in my Dream Team. He looked at me with that great mischievous glint in his eye and said, 'Big Man, it is one of my greatest honours!' He is a wind-up merchant, a guy that, like Jinky and Bertie Auld, just has such a terrific zest for life.

I told him I couldn't have a selection like this without him and in all honesty I have adapted the side to make sure the name Lennox appeared there, it was always in my mind to do that. There is no question that he could have played down the middle but I think when you look in the pages ahead at the players I have selected in the two striking roles then you will understand my thought process with this pick.

It always makes me laugh when I'm sitting talking football with the Lions and one of them will slaughter the man they nicknamed 'Lemon' and call him 'The Outsider'. Bobby was born and raised in the Ayrshire town of Saltcoats and he still lives there, thirty miles from Celtic Park. Lemon? Where did that come from? Was it because he made the guys who marked him look like lemons? Turns out it was a misprint from a newspaper that somehow managed to call him Bobby Lemon. Willie Wallace spotted this, called him Lemon and it stuck!

There is also that memorable stat of the entire team who won in Lisbon being born within thirty miles of the ground and it exists because of Bobby Lennox, the Ayr-shireman. The rest of them were Glaswegians and they take the mickey out of him saying the tag for that team would have been 'all born within ten miles of Celtic Park' if it wasn't for him! I love that.

When you study the Lions in depth it is interesting to see how many of them considered their Celtic careers to have been going nowhere until big Jock arrived on the scene at the Park. Bobby was no different – they were on the brink of flogging him to Falkirk for a giveaway fee before Stein got his hands on a talent that he grew to cherish. Lennox had blistering pace to expose defenders from wide positions and he had such a fantastic eye for goal. When Bobby had scored two or three goals he wanted four or five – he shared that selfish trait with Henrik Larsson and all the truly great strikers have it.

Sometimes if I had played in a game and I got on the sheet after fifteen minutes I had this little lazy habit of thinking that I had done my job and scored my goal. I had worked to get it, started the game well and I was rattling into people. Then I would notch one and I would rest on my laurels. There's no question in my mind that there were times when I did that in the Hoops. It was subconscious and I didn't mean to do it, but the fact is that I did and I know it. That's frustrating when I think about it now I am retired because this year I had a new tattoo etched on my right arm with 110 to celebrate my Celtic goals tally. I already have the crest there and I wouldn't have done that for any other club. That new piece of ink, though, could have had even more goals to celebrate on it if I hadn't dropped my game too often.

The truly great players, like my hero Ian Rush, Larsson or this man Bobby Lennox, have a mindset that simply will not allow them to settle for one or even two goals in a match. If they feel there are five to be had then they go and they hunt for those five. I used to watch Henrik in games when we were cruising it and he would be tearing around closing the goalkeeper down in the ninety-fourth minute when I was thinking about my shower! We would be 4-0 up and he was driven by this unbelievable hunger to go and get a fifth. That's what I believe separates the greats from the mere mortals like myself.

I was a top player but I was NOT a great, not in my eyes. There were times when I did great things when I was playing at my best but the true greats are the likes of Steven Gerrard and Paul Gascoigne who produce it time and again when it matters most. Lennox was like that. The word 'great' is used far too often, but Bobby merited it. If Bobby had the attitude of John Hartson he would still have been in our 100 Goals Club but he would have half of the 273 goals he scored for the Hoops. Instead he is up there with the legends because of one key word in football: attitude.

He played in a wonderful side which obviously helped him, but I think if you look at his career you will see a home truth running through it. He produced on the big occasions and when it came to the Old Firm games or the Cup finals the Lions knew they could rely on him to score.

Pace is such a vital commodity in the modern game and that's why Lennox would have survived and thrived in this era. He had electric acceleration and I think with the solid base this Dream Team has in defence and with Murdoch and McStay as the creative forces driving us on, then we can afford the flair and trickery of Jimmy Johnstone on the right and the attacking threat of Lennox on the left.

There are two quotes that sum Lennox up and they come from the mouths of two men with a whole lot more authority on Bobby's greatness than I could ever have:

'If I'd had Lennox in my team I could have played forever.

He was one of the best strikers I have ever seen.'
                                  – *Sir Bobby Charlton,*
                         ex-Manchester United and England

'The Scotsman who gave me the most trouble was Bobby Lennox. My testimonial at the Bernabeu was against Celtic as, of course, they were the European Cup holders in 1967. I will always remember the stadium rising to Jimmy Johnstone but I admired Lennox greatly.'
                         – *Real Madrid legend Alfredo di Stefano*

That tells you enough, although clearly one of the Celtic directors didn't give Lemon the same level of respect. In 1968 Bobby won the Bronze Boot as he was third top goalscorer in European football. Scandalously, the club never told him about this accolade and one of the board members jetted off to get the award at a lavish ceremony and handed it to Bobby at a pre-match dinner at Celtic Park!

Bobby's goalscoring record means that you would find it so very difficult to leave him out of the team. It demands that he be in there and you fashion a role for him. He is an interesting mix too, Lennox, when you are lucky enough to talk to him. There is so much fun in him, he has these laughing eyes when he tells you all the tales of what him and Jinky used to get up to on American tours with the Lions, and all the rest of it. To be honest, I really don't envy the job their skipper Billy McNeill had in keeping control of the lot of them and making sure they stayed out of big Jock's way! Yet when the chat turns to the game, to his craft as a striker, Bobby is deadly serious when he explains how he learned to use the attributes he had to exploit defences and score goals.

Still, though, when you are getting close to heaping praise on him for what he achieved he will find a way to deflect it all, shrugging and saying, 'I always remember when we beat Real Madrid in that di Stefano testimonial that all the papers had been full of how the Spaniards would show they were the best team in Europe and not us. Well, I think we proved a point that night. Who scored? Er, Lennox . . . after Jimmy Johnstone had beaten about fourteen players to set me up!'

Lennox is the sixth Lisbon Lion in my line-up and that tells you something about the job Stein and his dressing-room lieutenant McNeill did in focusing all those different talents into such a well-oiled machine that could simply control a game like that 1967 European Cup final against the legendary Inter Milan.

They love all the laughs and the gags and the stories, that team, but behind it all with men like Lennox is this steely resolve that shows you they were determined to be the best they could be. They didn't want to let down Jock and they didn't want to embarrass big Billy, who was their leader. That's why they were so successful, they were a band of brothers, and that's the phrase I keep coming back to. Look at Lennox, who is still best mates and golf buddies with Stevie Chalmers, who he played up front with. It's forty-five years since they were scampering around that field in Lisbon but they are still such a huge part of each other's lives. I love that about them.

They are a special group of men, and from Brother Walfrid to Willie Maley to Jimmy McGrory, Celtic have a rich and amazing history. Yet for me the modern-day Hoops were born the day Billy McNeill scored the goal that won the 1965 Scottish Cup final against Dunfermline. McGrory had been the manager through the first three rounds of that competition but Jock took over and got the club over the line in the Cup and all of a sudden the tide was turning in Glasgow and the balance of power was shifting. From then on Lennox – who, if you look in the pictures, stoops down to let Billy in to head the winner – was at the heart of something special. In 1967 there would be the European Cup glory run then Lisbon. People often forget that three years later the team reached the final again only to lose 2-1 to Feyenoord.

People may try to emulate the team spirit the Lions had but you just can't. They are a unique team and that is why they have a stand named after them at Celtic Park now. They could be as big-time as they want to be, but Bobby exemplifies the Lions as a breed. They are gracious gentlemen and I count myself fortunate to have met so many of them. I think it comes from their working-class roots. Bobby, for instance, worked in the huge ICI plant in

Stevenston before he went to Celtic. He made boxes in a factory, it was repetitive, boring work and the minute he got to play football for a living he appreciated every second of it. Still, when you have won the right to play for Celtic you have to have what it takes to hold onto it.

Living as a player in the Celtic attack brings its pressures as a footballer. I have a wry smile when I'm having a quiet pint sometimes and people have a conversation and they'll say, 'It must have been great getting all those chances when you were dominating games.' Listen, the demands of playing in that position for this club have taken some players in, chewed them up and spat them back out again. Guys like Tony Cascarino, who cost £1.1 million in the Liam Brady era and had a decent career everywhere else but then he toiled in the Hoops. Now that can be down to the team you played in but it can also be down to the pressures that are placed upon you at the Old Firm. You get players who are terrific at, say, Hibs or Hearts and they go to Celtic and the expectation level changes. The rules are that you have to win every game. You are there to be shot at, every game is live on TV, you are back three pages of every paper, you are on internet message boards for hours after every match. You are the centre of attention – question is, can you cope?

Bobby Lennox could, season after season after season. This is Scotland's equivalent of playing for Manchester United, in my eyes. I had experienced that a little at Arsenal who I consider to be London's biggest club. They are not the richest but I see them as the biggest. You could feel the pressure there, you had to have the cocky mentality of an Ian Wright, the ice-cool calm of Dennis Bergkamp, to cope with the heat of being relied on for goals there. I had that in me and I could cope at Celtic but I have seen it swallow players up. Not Lennox. Year after year Bobby coped with threats to his position but in the main until the twilight days of his career he always kept his starting jersey because he raised his levels. It's like the first time I went to play for Wales and Ryan Giggs was firing balls in to me. I thought, 'I can't miscontrol this, he's used to playing with Keane and Beckham and he rattles balls into Ruud van Nistelrooy every day in training. Control the ****ing thing!'

I think that's where people struggle at Celtic and that's where guys like Lennox were critical, even after the glory days of Lisbon. He set a benchmark of what was required for guys like Lou Macari, Dixie Deans and Kenny Dalglish. They looked at Bobby and they knew what they had to live up to. It was like the day Roy Keane first walked onto the training field in my final year at Celtic. Every player that morning, I can assure you, had an extra spring in their step and an extra zip to their work.

Bobby is one of those players who deep down is respected and admired by the blue half of Glasgow. I like to think I have that too nowadays. The Rangers fans realise I turned up for my medical there in good faith, it was their club who decided I wasn't fit enough to pull on one of their jerseys. With Lennox I think they just all wish he had played for them. It showed the dignity there is at times between two of football's bitterest rivals when you consider that a tackle from John Greig broke Bobby's leg in November 1976. In lesser men that would have sparked bad blood and bitterness, but not Bobby. He forgave Greigy, who was one of the first men to visit him in hospital afterwards, and the incident was put into perspective. People don't forget conduct like that when you hang up your boots.

I know Bobby Lennox worked with the Celtic reserves for a long spell and I think he left some of his magic behind for others to feed on. In those days there weren't the opportunities I have had to move on into the media world, but nothing would have stopped Bobby from staying on to work at Celtic anyhow. There is a Lennox legacy for me, and Kenny Dalglish always speaks so highly of him and the influence that he had on him on the way up and again that is the measure of the man. You need that as a front man, and when I got to play with Wales I got to play and train with my hero Ian Rush, which was almost surreal. I had pictures of this guy on my bedroom wall and here I was learning from him. He was a Welsh icon and the only reason I am a Liverpool fan is because of Ian Rush. He instigated my love for that club and I still look out for their result every Saturday because of him.

Lennox had that sort of effect on players too. It never ceases to amaze me that wherever you go in the world you can find a Celtic fan – naturally with a legend like Lennox, that goes one step further. When he quit Celtic at first he jetted out to America to play for Houston Hurricane. I'm told they still have a Celtic Supporters' Club named after him to this day. Fittingly, his old Lions pal Billy McNeill brought Bobby back into the fold at Paradise and he was part of the team the night Ten Men Won the League against Rangers in 1979. In all, Bobby's Celtic medal haul of eleven titles, eight Scottish Cups and five League Cups beats even that of Cesar. And he played in two European Cup finals. Ask him about losing that 1970 final to Feyenoord these days and he still shudders. 'Losing that night was the lowest point of my football career. It is the one big regret I have from my time at Celtic and I still think about it today.

'We could have been double European champions, two-time winners. The fact is, though, we just didn't play well on the night even though everybody had us as big favourites for that one.

'Guys who have been in that situation know what I am talking about. The European Cup final is one of the biggest games you can lose, I still don't like thinking about it.'

Yet the man had far more highs than he had lows. I mean, I have had good years in my career but the 1967 season that Bobby Lennox had would take some beating: he played for Scotland at Wembley against the 1966 World Cup winners, England, and he scored in a 3-2 win as Jim Baxter played keepie-uppie and took the mickey out of the Auld Enemy. He won the European Cup in Lisbon, then he went to play in Alfredo di Stefano's testimonial at Real Madrid and scored the winner. That's just a ticket to dreamland – you don't get seasons like that. I mean, look at that English side. They had all the legends playing for them but Baxter, Lennox and the rest tore them to ribbons that day. I have been able to sit with Bobby and talk about days like that and I treasure that.

I got 110 goals for Celtic but I know I am not a legend – nowhere near it. I was a pretty decent striker for the club but this fella? Well, he was a legend, and that's why Bobby Lennox is in my Celtic Dream Team.

10

GOALS IN PARADISE

When a keeper breaks *three fingers* trying to save one of your headers you have a right to call yourself a power-house of a centre-forward. Step forward, James Edward McGrory. When I first came to Celtic I heard the fans singing the name of James McGrory in that Willie Maley song and wondered who this guy had been. Why was he so special to a generation of supporters who'd never seen him play? I soon learned.

McGrory's story is remarkable, that's the only word for it. You can't score 472 in 445 appearances for Celtic and be considered anything other than that. Remarkable. For sixteen years after Maley brought him to the club from junior side St Roch's in 1921, Jimmy McGrory terrorised defences. That's the only word for it. I'd have loved to have seen films of him play but when you read the stories they are vivid enough.

Mr McGrory sounds like my type of striker, he'd break his jaw diving for a header to score a goal, and the press boys back then called him 'The Human Torpedo' because of the way he threw himself at crosses. That piece of folklore started when he launched himself at a cross to score a last-minute winner in the 1925 Scottish Cup final against Dundee. The Human Torpedo? I love that. Queen's Park keeper Jack Harkness, who'd go on to become a famous newspaper reporter, broke those fingers trying to stop a thumping McGrory header, and you have to marvel at a record that saw Jimmy crowned Celtic's top scorer for twelve seasons on the bounce. In 1927 and 1936 he stood looking down on the whole continent as the top scorer in Europe. The tallies for those seasons were forty-nine and fifty goals, which is an amazing strike rate.

When you look at the stories of Celtic players up to perhaps the 1970s there are too many who have paltry cap totals for there not to have been something in the minds of the Scotland selectors. I don't know enough about the impact of religion or people's prejudices in those times, or how the Irish roots of Celtic were looked at to make a certain statement on this. All I can do is look at the figures and feel that for someone who scored 472 goals in 445 games for Celtic, seven Scotland caps is just nonsense. Mind you, in one of them Mr McGrory scored a late winner against the English and the noise from 134,170 fans was so loud they called it 'The Hampden Roar'. That one stuck!

Another chord that struck me researching this book was that in 1928 my old club Arsenal tried to buy Jimmy McGrory in a £10,000 deal and the Celtic board were desperate to see him accept it. They were licking their lips and they must have been thinking of all that dough coming into the coffers but their star striker said thanks but no thanks. The history books will tell you that the Celtic directors were so livid with McGrory they paid him

LESS than his team-mates for the rest of his career. Can you imagine that? It's disgraceful, yet when McGrory found out he just shrugged. 'Well, it was worth it just to pull on those green and white Hoops.' It's when you ponder stories like that that you realise why even now, the 75th anniversary of Jimmy's retirement, we are all still singing his praises. A true Celtic legend.

Looking up Mr McGrory's background brought me to the list of Celtic's Top 10 Goalscorers. That top three of McGrory, Lennox and Larsson made me stop for a moment and think just how privileged I was to play alongside Henrik. As a guy who has so much pride in his 110 goals for Celtic, a glance at that Top 10 list is awe-inspiring. Underneath those top three there lie:

STEVIE CHALMERS (231 goals in 393 games)

I scored for Arsenal in that 1995 Cup Winners' Cup final against Real Zaragoza but we lost. I dreamed of scoring the winner for Celtic in the 2003 UEFA Cup final against FC Porto but my back injury cheated me out of the chance.

This guy will go to his grave as the man who scored the goal that won the European Cup for Celtic and it's fitting that honour lies with such a gentleman who sums up all that is good about the club. Don't ever look at that Lisbon goal and think it is a fluke. Stevie anticipates Bobby Murdoch's slightly mis-hit shot and he gambles on where to be to score. It's a striker's instinct but it is also something I know Stein trained the players on, being in there to pick up the scraps.

Again Stevie had a right to question why he wasn't used more by Scotland but when he did play he can also claim the accolade of having scored against Brazil. Anyhow, Stevie left Paradise with four titles, three Scottish Cups and four League Cups and I'd take that any day. Oh, and the European Cup winner's medal!

JIMMY QUINN (217 goals in 311 games)
Willie Maley had to persuade Jimmy Quinn, the shy son of a hard-working Irish family, that he was good enough to play for Celtic before he signed on Hogmanay in 1900. History tells you of a strong-running player with a bullet shot who I suppose had to be tagged 'The Mighty Quinn', and Jimmy helped Celtic to six titles on the spin in his time. Just as well Maley had the management *nous* to convince the former collier boy he was a player after all.

PATSY GALLACHER (192 goals in 464 games)
'The Mighty Atom.' Folklore says that this guy, born in the Celtic stronghold of Donegal, was one of the most gifted players ever to grace the club. Patsy was slim and frail but, like Jimmy Johnstone five decades later, Gallacher soon showed his team-mates that he could be trusted with the ball and no-one would kick him out of a game. He tormented defenders with his dribbling, like Jinky, and he was no circus trick player. He set them up and he scored them, there was a purpose to his work.

Gallacher came to Scotland as part of a dirt-poor Irish family looking to make a name for himself, and he did that. Mission accomplished. There's this great story on the great Celtic Wiki site that tells you of Patsy playing in the blue of Rangers in a benefit match for his Ibrox pal, Andy Cunningham. Now I failed a medical at Ibrox, but try and conjure the image of me in a Rangers shirt now. It just wouldn't look right! Patsy clearly thought the same because at the end of the game he took off his jersey to reveal that he was wearing the Hoops underneath. It says even the Gers fans laughed. Imagine if you tried that now!

Patsy's departure from Celtic again has echoes of boardrooms and management not realising what they had and trying to stint on the money. Boss Maley told the press Gallacher was retiring in 1926, and a raging Patsy said he knew nothing about it and went on to play for Falkirk for another six years. The reason for the bust-up was wages, and it is sad how often that cropped up before the club changed its attitudes. Gallacher's place in Celtic's history, though, was long since assured.

JOHN HUGHES (188 goals in 416 games)
The original 'Feed the Bear' man before Roy Aitken ever appeared on the scene! Before Jock Stein changed Celtic's world with that 1965 Scottish Cup triumph over Dunfermline, big Yogi was a light in the gloom for the Hoops fans. He was such a powerful presence and invaluable on the heavy pitches they had in winters then as he ploughed through the muck, scoring goal after goal.

Like me in Seville, when his team's crowning glory came, John was injured. He sat it out in Lisbon and that must have been heartbreaking because he played in five of the nine European games that season. He is a Lion and should always be remembered as one.

There is some ill luck running through John's career, though. For instance, he was brilliant in the 1968-69 Treble season but injured for both Cup finals. In 1970 he haunted Jack Charlton at Hampden and scored a fantastic header in the European Cup semi-final win over Leeds United.

Yogi was a huge character and it is said that when Jock Stein agreed his departure to Crystal Palace it was a move the big man didn't want, which is a shame but football is a cruel game at times. The affection for John from the Celtic fans, though, will always be there.

SANDY McMAHON (171 goals in 217 games)
Sandy McMahon played in a bygone age at the turn of the last century but with a strike rate like his, he must have been something special. They called him 'The Duke' because the French president at the time was called Patrice de Mac-Mahon. Great nickname. Sandy was tempted south in 1892 by the lure of money at Nottingham Forest – the game had just gone pro down there then – but the pull of Celtic brought him back to sparkle again for Willie Maley.

JIMMY McMENEMY (168 goals in 456 games)
Another player in that six-in-a-row title run from 1905 to 1910, McMenemy was another striker of note and carried the nicknamed 'Napoleon'. Jimmy is a great quiz question because his son John won a Scottish Cup medal for Celtic in 1927 and Lawrie McMenemy, the former Southampton boss, is a distant relation.

That is my nod to the history of the club I love. I didn't see many of these players play but their stories are brought alive in all the great books and websites that make Celtic so different from any other football club. In my hunt for my dream pairing up front, they are all candidates. As is any player who, like me, carries the distinction of playing for Arsenal and Celtic – two very special football clubs who will always occupy a place in my heart. Charlie Nicholas grew up next door to my fellow *Scottish Sun* columnist Jim Duffy, a guy whose football knowledge and insights I have come to respect so much. They remain close and it still tickles me when they call each other Charles and James, as if their mums are still watching them and telling them not to shorten what they were christened with.

Back at the start when Charlie was first making his name as a Celtic player, Billy McNeill got pelters for holding him back. When he was unleashed in August 1980 he exploded onto the scene, the newspapers quickly called him 'the Cannonball Kid' and he scored thirteen goals in his first twelve games for the top team. The story of his first spell in the Hoops is one of an unbelievable talent, in my opinion – helped by the unselfish Frank McGarvey beside him – who grew too big for Glasgow and a transfer south was inevitable. There was a circus around Charlie in his best season when fifty-three goals in total won him so much attention, but the sadness is that whilst he won double Player of the Year, the team lost the title to Dundee United. His class, though, and his departure at the age of just twenty-one meant he would be sorely missed.

By that time, however, Charlie had already had a bad leg break and maybe he realised just what a precarious life we all have at the top level. It can all be snatched away from you in the blink of an eye with one savage tackle. I for one, having made as many moves as I did, could never decry any player for trying to better their contract or look for a new challenge. I can't class the Nicholas years at Arsenal as being wasted either. He came back with a League Cup winner's medal to Aberdeen for a couple of years before a second spell at Celtic. Yet I think it is fair to say there are always going to be questions over Charlie's choice of move when the world was at his feet. He went for the bright lights of London when Liverpool were the best team in Europe at the time and Manchester United had their own appeal too. With me, as you know by now, it would have been Anfield every time – they were my boyhood heroes – but I'm sure Charlie had his reasons.

One thing is for sure, it was his choice to make and whatever you think of Charlie's career in the Hoops he will defend himself and I respect that fearlessness. Charlie is not frightened to voice his opinion now and he has got on the wrong side of a lot of Celtic fans by doing that. He is in the 100 Club with me, scoring over a century of goals for the club, and I really respect every player who has hit the mark because I know how hard it is. So we share something special in playing for both Arsenal and Celtic, and he remains a huge favourite with the Gunners fans even though he didn't play in a particularly successful side. I'm not sure I would have wanted to carry a nickname like 'Champagne Charlie', but sometimes you have no say in that.

He was top notch, though, Charlie. If I had a memory that I carry of him it is of quick feet and such an alert brain to find the chance and to finish. He was quality and one thing I always say to those who criticise the Gunners is that Arsenal don't sign poor players. They just don't.

Charlie helped win a League Cup for Arsenal and the fans still remember that but if I am honest I don't think he admired me the way I might have admired him as a footballer. He was a big fan of Sutton and Larsson and he made that known in his columns in the *Daily Express*. Any player who tells you he doesn't read the papers is a liar, they are always there in the dining room in the morning or in the physio's room when you are getting a rub. We read them alright. Charlie would always back Chris and Henrik, and that got my back up a bit. They were great players but I was in there on merit and I was achieving the same things. When you have someone in the media who you feel is always against you then it gets to you and I would be lying if I didn't say that it got to me with Charlie. It got to me alright and he was motivating me to get in and score more goals and prove a point.

Charlie rubs the Celtic fans up the wrong way now more often than not, the same way Craig Burley does. They criticise the club a lot and they seem to revel in upsetting the fans. That is their way, though, and they have made a very good living out of the media.

Me? I try to strike a balance because I can't go to the lengths of putting the boot into Celtic. I already have half of Glasgow that can't stand me as it is! I want to come back and still be fondly remembered by the other half. I make no excuses for that. I have walked through Glasgow Airport and been called a Fenian b****** and all the rest of it, and it's not nice. I wouldn't be happy if the Celtic fans were giving me abuse too, because that is MY team. The one I played for and scored for, the one I love and want to come back to and be able to watch as a fan. Yet Craig and Charlie don't seem to think the same way about their relationship with the fans, and that's just the way they choose to live in the media. I can't do it, I can't lambast the club I took a very good living out of for five of the happiest years of my career. That wouldn't be right.

Charlie Nicholas the player, though, earns his right to be in this chapter with the legend that is James McGrory, the names of Stevie Chalmers, Patsy Gallacher and the rest. Not including McGrory as one of my strikers is bound to cause huge debate but I didn't see that legendary man play and I had to make a choice. That choice is King Kenny.

Rangers must regret every day not signing Kenny Dalglish, who grew up dreaming of wearing a light blue jersey, not a green-and-white hooped one. The day the Celtic scout came to talk to Kenny he was running into his bedroom in his flat near Ibrox tearing the Gers posters off the walls! That, to me, suggests Celtic were doing their job and Rangers weren't doing theirs – certainly when it came to Kenneth Mathieson Dalglish.

Kenny made the hard trek up from the juniors at Cumbernauld to become a player that the Kop called 'King Kenny'. It's some journey when you think about it. He was just class and he's scored 100 goals north and south of the border and has that record 102 caps for Scotland. He's a legend as a player and as a manager in my eyes after he won the Double at Liverpool as player-boss and the Premier League at Blackburn Rovers and I have to say that it surprises me that Scotland never came calling for him as their international manager. Mind you, could the SFA have coped with him? As a Liverpool fan, Dalglish is one of my real heroes and I remember talking to Ian Rush about him. Rushie talks of him so fondly as both a player and a person and he described the partner-ship they had at their peak to me in one word: telepathic.

It was like Chris Sutton and Henrik Larsson the season before I arrived at Celtic, like Kevin Keegan and John Toshack in their heyday at Liverpool. They knew each other's game inside-out. Kenny would get up against a defender and stick that big arse of his out and no-one could get the ball off him, he was one of the best ever at shielding the ball. Then he had the class to find the weight of pass to slide his partner in and nine times out of ten Rushie wouldn't have to break stride to get his shot in on goal.

I admired the way Kenny protected the ball because I see shielding it as an art. I always liked to have the XXL shorts on, to be honest, because I felt then I was a beast to reckon with. I remember having a conversation with Gazza, who said he always felt better playing half a stone heavy. He felt then that with the skill he had, NO-ONE could dispossess him. I felt comfortable and strong seven pounds over and I have always felt there was a bit of that with Kenny.

My strength was my strength, holding the ball up. I could keep two players away from it and there is an art to it. All it takes for me to lose it is one poke of a defender's boot and then the manager is screaming at me to get hold of it. I learned from watching Dalglish, because he was brilliant at it. He kept it away from people and then he had the ability on the half-turn to play someone in. The great thing about Dalglish as a footballer was that you couldn't pigeon-hole him as a number 9 or as a guy who played in the role behind the strikers. He was just King Kenny, HE decided where he played.

Rush and Dalglish have to be up there with the greatest strike partnerships the English game has ever seen. I always loved watching Alan Shearer and Teddy Sheringham with England too and felt they could have been some double act if a club manager could somehow have financed that one at the right time. The best combination I had in my career was with Henrik, and I would have to put him down as the best striker that I played with. The strange thing is that the season Larsson left the Hoops was my best at the club in terms of goalscoring.

Kenny was an all-round footballer who prided himself on doing the simple things perfectly and then being able to produce the piece of magic his team needed to win the game. Dalglish didn't have electrifying pace but he had enough to get him away from players, and that was enough for him to have in his locker because he played the first five yards in his head. That's how far ahead he was of ordinary players. It was all about anticipating where the ball was going to land with players like Kenny.

I can pay no higher compliment to Sheringham and Kevin Phillips than to say there is a little bit of Dalglish in their footballing DNA. They have the *nous* to know where that ball is going to drop and it's not a fluke that it happens time and again. When everyone else is watching the ball, they are getting ready off-camera for the chance no-one can see developing. It's a sixth sense, and Dalglish had it. All the great ones do.

The way to judge a player is to ask those who played with him and against him how good he was. Now I respect the fans' awards and the Football Writers' Player of the Year honours, but for me the one you really want to win is Players' Player of the Year. And I don't say that just because I shared the SPFA Player of the Year with Rangers' Fernando Ricksen in 2005 – honest! I'm not a fan of awards like Player of the Year even in kids' football because you are trying to put eight-year-old boys into a team and teach them an ethic of togetherness, then you mark one of them out as the special one. Yet if you get them to vote for each other, to recognise what each other brings to the table . . . that's different. That's your peers recognising you and that's what Dalglish had in spades when you speak to anyone who marked him or played alongside him.

I have loved speaking with Alan Hansen, Ian Rush and Charlie Nicholas about Kenny, and they all rave about what it was like to get on his wavelength and play football with him. It was the same in my team with Henrik. We all thought Larsson was a genius, we all idolised him and thought he was the greatest thing to ever happen to Celtic. I am being honest here – grown men felt like that because we knew he could dig us out of any hole we got ourselves into.

Kenny proved himself at Celtic and the way his star was rising the offers from England were always going to come. In the end Dalglish did what Paul McStay didn't do, he took the plunge and moved south. I sympathise with that and think he probably had to at the time to further his career. Dalglish felt the chance might pass him by and he took it to go on and become a legend for the red half of Merseyside. I would argue that McStay had the ability to do that for a Manchester United if he elected to. They just made different choices.

Kenny was Kevin Keegan's successor in the number 7 jersey and that carried so much pressure with it but in my eyes, as close as they are in stature in the game, I think Dalglish had the edge. Keegan worked so hard on making himself a player and he turned Newcastle United around again in one of the great football stories of recent times. Yet I always felt Keegan was a manufactured player in some way, whereas Kenny had God-given genius.

The footballing loves of my life are Swansea City, Liverpool and Celtic and the only black mark Dalglish has in the hero stakes is that he somehow didn't get around to playing for the Swans. Sort it out, Kenny! Privately, Dalglish is a far different person from the one the media and the public see on their television screens. Under scrutiny he will always back his players when they are under fire, the way Luis Suarez was in the racism controversy last season. I know he doesn't have much time for the modern-day media because he disagrees with the culture of putting players up on a pedestal then bringing them crashing down. His players admire his determination to protect them but I accept that from outside the Suarez situation didn't look good. I'm just explaining what I see as the Dalglish psyche.

I'm sure the flak that Liverpool faced for their handling of the Suarez affair was a contributing factor to the decision of the American owners to sack Kenny as manager and make way for Brendan Rodgers to be tempted away from my hometown club Swansea. Yet I feel that was unfair in the sense that Liverpool had won the Carling Cup and Andy Carroll had that header late on against Cheslea that should have counted to take the FA Cup final into extra-time when Liverpool would have had all the momentum.

Yes, Liverpool were ninth in the Premier League, which wasn't good enough, but it was a work in progress and to sack him after a season was very harsh. I never thought that they would sack Kenny Dalglish at Anfield – for me, he is Mr Liverpool. But they did it and now the club will have to move on.

As a manager at Celtic I hope his legacy is not tainted by the failure of the Dream Team project when he came in as Director of Football and made his old Liverpool player, John Barnes, his coach. I don't think that should leave sour grapes in how he is regarded as a player. I pray the Celtic and Liverpool fans remember him as the player he was and for the joy he gave them. I am sure the whole Barnes episode will gnaw away at Kenny though, he is a proud man and, believe me, he has a real affinity with the Hoops. It will have hurt him to see that project fail. He saw something in Barnes when John was a player at Liverpool, something that suggested to Kenny that this articulate and gifted footballer he built a side round would someday be a top coach. Maybe he would have been but, in hindsight, Celtic can be a brutal environment for your first major job. There was no way back for John after the Scottish Cup defeat at home to Inverness Caledonian Thistle. From that night on he was going the same way as Liam Brady and Lou Macari before him and Tony Mowbray after him. Out the exit door.

Kenny has come through so much as a man after the horrors of the Hillsborough disaster when ninety-six Liverpool fans perished in a crush at the 1989 FA Cup semi-final against Nottingham Forest. Remember, that came only four years after what Kenny's club went through at Heysel when thirty-three Juventus fans and six Liverpool fans died in similar scenes before the 1985 European Cup final in Belgium. After Hillsborough,

Dalglish was at the funerals of every fan that perished and I think people then saw the true measure of the man. He carried an entire city on his shoulders during some traumatic times.

The thing that keeps you at Celtic and Rangers when you are at the peak of your powers as a footballer is the Old Firm games. That is not me belittling the SPL or the other clubs, it's just the truth. They are ferocious occasions, real stick-out matches in your life that you can tell your grandchildren you played in. They test you as a player and a person, they test your mettle and your character. Can you cope with the abuse and the hatred? Can you shine in that environment? Can you play under those terms? Can you be the difference? I scored four goals in a row in that fixture, and Dalglish was the same, he thrived on it. So that keeps you in Glasgow and Europe lures you too. But there comes a time when England is tugging at you and in the end Kenny couldn't resist the pull.

In three out of my five seasons at Celtic I played in the Champions League and it kept me there and happy but I understand what lured Dalglish away. Kenny left Celtic in 1977 and within a year he was scoring the winner in the European Cup final against FC Bruges at Wembley. Much as it might pain the Celtic fans for me to argue this point, I would say on balance you have to say he made the right decision. Kenny gave Liverpool so much and my favourite moment was the goal that won the Double at Chelsea in 1986 when he took the ball on his chest and battered in that title-clinching volley. He did score a great header on the run against Wales to take Scotland to Argentina 1978, but I don't want to talk about that one! His international record of thirty goals remains the best ever, alongside Denis Law, and no-one can doubt what he gave to his nation in those 102 caps.

As I say, if you know the history then the choice of two all-time strikers for the Hoops is a perilous one to have to make, especially as everyone who plays in that position for the club in a way operates in the shadow of James McGrory.

Kenny Dalglish, though, is the one I saw play. He epitomised what you want to be in that position and that's why he is in my Celtic Dream Team.

11

THE KING OF KINGS

He is the King of Kings, he would have been a star for the Lisbon Lions, he is Henrik Larsson and I was honoured to play beside him. So far on this journey only Jimmy Johnstone could be inked into my Heaven's Eleven without dispute, but when you have scored 242 goals in 315 games for Celtic as Henrik did, then I feel you too should earn that right.

I have now selected Celtic's three greatest number 7s: Jinky, Henrik and Kenny Dalglish. The big question I have to ask myself is, who would get to wear that jersey for my team? Truth is, they all merit it but I would hand it to Henrik. Someone should have solved this dilemma for me and retired the jersey before now and then I wouldn't have this problem. It would go to Larsson for me, though, and I would have to suffer Kenny giving me a verbal battering for it. I just had the pleasure of playing with Henrik and that's what swings it for me.

When you look back now at the £650,000 Wim Jansen paid Feyenoord to invoke a contract clause and bring Henrik to Celtic – after a bitter dispute with the Dutch club – it has to go down as one of the biggest transfer heists in the club's 125-year history. Together Jansen and Larsson stopped ten in a row for Rangers, but in the three years before the gaffer Martin O'Neill arrived at Celtic, Henrik went through some hellish times and people too often forget that.

Dr Jozef Venglos' reign did bring a kindred spirit for Henrik to link up with in Lubomir Moravčik, but Celtic were being outstripped in the transfer market by Rangers and they were toiling. Henrik had an exciting partnership with Mark Viduka when it clicked, but the big Aussie was at war with the club – and the world at times, it seemed – too often for the double act to click as it should have. Venglos bit the dust, then in came the ill-fated John Barnes–Kenny Dalglish era and Henrik suffered a horrific leg break in Lyon that left him on the sidelines for eight months and would have finished a lesser player without the core of steel he had inside him. He returned in time to play in Euro 2000 for Sweden and, more importantly if you are a Celtic fan, to be fit for the start of the Martin O'Neill era at the club. I was down south then but can vividly recall watching this dreadlocked genius take a knockdown from Chris Sutton before running from half-way, nutmegging a defender and then dinking the most brilliant of chips over the head of hapless Rangers keeper, Stefan Klos. Celtic battered them 6-2 in the opening Old Firm derby and I thought, 'Wow, what a player.'

Celtic roared to the Treble, Henrik won the European Golden Boot and was named the Scottish Football Writers' Player of the Year and Martin O'Neill decided to go out that summer and sign some big Welshman called John Hartson! Henrik had a huge reputation when I came to the club at first and all I seemed to hear was the talk of this partnership – Sutton and Larsson, Sutton and Larsson. I went to sleep at night with those names swirling around in my head and fearing that I wouldn't get a game because of them.

Even inside the Celtic camp they had seen Henrik see off the likes of Harald Brattbakk, Tommy Johnson and Mark Burchill, but now they had found the perfect foil for him. The season before I arrived they had scored sixty-six goals between them, Henrik got fifty-three and Chris hit thirteen, and the team had won the Treble.

Sutton had been a £10 million signing for Chelsea and he had won the English Premier League with Blackburn Rovers. He was a proven force in English football, the real deal. The players saw Chris as a great signing, not just for Celtic Football Club, but for Henrik Larsson. The players wanted Henrik to be happy, to have the partnership he deserved because they knew what he could do. Now here was the big Welsh fella coming in and I did wonder how on earth I could split that partnership up. The answer was that, at first, I didn't. I really rated Sutty and I soon learned that Henrik was close to a god amongst the fans. In one of my first games in the Champions League qualifiers we won 3-1 at Ajax. I'd been on the bench, Chris had scored, and I was very much still the new boy.

On the bus on the way to the airport I was content enough because I had made it to Celtic but deep down inside I had this burning desire to play. I wanted to be a starter. Martin sat next to me and said to me on the bus, 'I know you are looking at that front two. I know you are recognising the feel-good factor they have created, the

Treble they have won, but you WILL get into this team. Just bear with me, and when you get into this team you will have the crowd eating out of your hand.'

If I am honest, I thought that was just a manager trying to butter up a £6 million signing and keep him sweet. Yet he was true to his word and he got me into the team, but I took time to adapt. I had a great tussle with big Marvin Andrews in a 0-0 draw at Livingston and I was enjoying it but the goals wouldn't come. I felt pressure beside Henrik because I knew Chris had made so many goals for his strike partner and I knew too that nothing would change the fact that Henrik was the star man here. So I had to get things straight in my head, we played around him and I had to find a way to make that work.

Then I got my hat-trick against Dundee United in a 5-1 win at our place to get myself off and running. The manager could see we had something and we developed a system then with Chris Sutton in time adapting to his European role in midfield. In the dressing room Henrik was a reserved character but on the training field you saw where the greatness came from – he was a ridiculously hard worker. He was thorough and determined and he knew what he could achieve for himself but he was a team player. None more so than in the Seville season.

There are two things that will always kill me about that momentous season: one is that despite playing twelve games out of fourteen on the Euro run, injury would rob me of a place in the final; the second is that although we gave the club their pride back on the European stage we lost the title on the final day and ended up trophyless. Henrik, in particular, deserved better.

Footballers are selfish creatures though, and that night in the broiling Stadio Olimpico I was hurting for myself, badly. Yet what lifted me throughout those gut-wrenching 120 minutes was watching someone I trained and laughed with every day announce himself as a truly world-class player. As if there had ever really been any doubt. After that match I took time out to reflect on this special striker I was working beside and I recalled that I had felt the same way about Ian Wright at Arsenal, who I loved as a front man. With Wrighty, though, it all revolved around HIM scoring, he was really down if he didn't hit the net.

Henrik wasn't like that, his selfishness, if you can call it that, came from this streak where he would want to score five and not just one if he got hot in a game. Us mere mortals might settle for one or two but that is what set him apart. It was never enough.

Larsson's right to be considered above all others in this chapter is hammered home when you ponder the candidates who, all too fleetingly, captured the hearts of the Celtic supporters. I call Pierre van Hooijdonk 'Mr What-Might-Have-Been'. He could have been a legend like Henrik but wages bust-ups and feuds with Fergus McCann saw him heading for the exit door before his time. Pierre had a contract offer that was £7,000 a week on the table and he called it slave labour pay that might be good enough for a homeless person, but not for a top-class striker. That was crass – Glasgow people hate that sort of arrogant stuff – it wasn't his cleverest interview by a long chalk and I think it stuck in the minds of a lot of people.

What a player he was, though. For such a big man he had fantastic individual ability, he could take free-kicks like you wouldn't believe. He was 6'5" yet he had the feet of a little, dinky midfield player and a touch to die for. He wasn't aggressive for such a towering presence but for me his biggest quality was his touch and the way he could turn and play others in or create something for himself. The Celtic fans deserved to see more of di Canio and van Hooijdonk because they should have gone on to be legends for the club.

I would be very proud to be mentioned in the same breath as Paolo, Pierre, Andreas Thom and Jorge Cadete in terms of ability, but they came and went so quickly. They burned so brightly in such a short space of time at the club, but just think of the impact they could have had. Van Hooijdonk at first flourished in the Hoops under the watchful gaze of Tommy Burns. He scored thirty-two goals in his first full season and also netted the 1995 Scottish Cup final winner against Airdrie that ended six barren years without a trophy.

Wee Fergus loved those Three Amigos, as he called them, didn't he? Van Hooijdonk, di Canio and Jorge Cadete all went to war with him and Jorge ended up back home in Portugal with a canary called Fergus! Jorge always seemed destined to be followed by controversy after a bitter row over his registration saw him cooling his heels for six weeks before he was allowed to play. A clash that eventually cost the then SFA chief executive, Jim Farry, his job. Cadete and van Hooijdonk were a potent partnership and the Portuguese hitman was a superb finisher with a killer burst of pace. He was class. Again he was gone all too soon. If he had hung around he could have partnered Henrik up front, and I really think that would have been something else to see.

One player who had the chance, all too briefly, to form a double act with Larsson was Mark Viduka, but again the fans' memories of him are soured because of the way his stay at the club ended. The big Aussie had so much going for him, a powerful presence, heading ability and a terrific touch for a guy who was such a big unit. Henrik's leg break in Lyon saw Viduka taking on the mantle and he hit the goal trail to win the Players' Player of the Year award. There had been problems when he signed at first for Celtic, though, and when I talk to fans about him now, I get this sense that they were suspicious of big Mark and his motives at times. The humiliating Scottish Cup loss at home to Inverness Caledonian Thistle was the beginning of the end for him, though, as a seething row with the coaching staff allegedly saw him refuse to come out for the second half.

Celtic won a League Cup but Viduka was already eyeing a move to Spain or England, and he got his wish with a £6 million transfer to Leeds United. If he looks back on his career I think he might regret not listening to Martin O'Neill and sticking around. As it was, the gaffer used that £6 million to land Chris Sutton from Chelsea – and the rest is history.

Those guys, if I am honest, are simply the pretenders to the throne – there is only one King of Kings and I've never felt that nickname was too much hype for Henrik. Listen, they've had Martin Dahlin, Tomas Brolin and the rest from Sweden, but their best export has been Henrik. I include Zlatan Ibrahimovic in that and he has gone for £140 million in transfers in his life after his latest move to Paris Saint-Germain in summer of 2011. On the international front, the Swedes voted Henrik their greatest player of the last fifty years and he scored goals at three World Cup finals – 1994, 2002 and 2006 – and two European Championships in 2000 and 2004. Take that alongside thirty-seven international goals in 106 caps and you have some career to reflect on.

The question I am asked most frequently about Henrik is: 'What was he really like?' I find that a very difficult one to answer. He kept the press at arm's length and I know some of the media boys found him prickly to deal with. I didn't see that side, he was great in the dressing room, but while I know people always want to find out about Henrik the man, he was just a private guy. If I'm honest, we didn't mix that much away from the club, I just wanted to learn as much as I could from him as a footballer. That was the way it was when you worked alongside him. Even Ronaldinho at Barcelona later in his career would say, 'With Henrik leaving us at the end of the season, this club is losing a great scorer, no question. But I am also losing a great friend.

'Henrik was my idol and now that I am playing next to him it is fantastic. He is a real friend and that is a pleasure. I just want to enjoy the remaining time he has with us rather than dwell on what we will be missing when he's gone. I haven't tried to convince Henrik to stay at Barcelona. I respect him so much that I can't try to influence his decision.'

It was hard for Henrik in the goldfish bowl that is Glasgow, though. If he went into town he was like the Pied Piper, there would be people following him every-where. We were stars, but he was a genuine superstar. He was and he remains a god to the Celtic fans, Celtic's answer to Alan Shearer in Newcastle. He wasn't just the best player, he was the best trainer at the club, and there is no doubt in my mind that he could have played for the Lisbon Lions.

I was a goalscorer myself and I think now that Henrik would tell you that Chris was a better foil for him – I liked creating goals for him but my psyche as a footballer was all about scoring as well. I thought about goals all the time, whereas Chris also loved to be the creator. I had played with Wrighty and he was special and I shared the same pitch with Bergkamp at the Gunners and with Giggs with Wales, but Henrik was up there with the very best of them. He scored the goal that got us to Seville with the winner in Boavista and then those two unbelievable headers in that 3-2 UEFA Cup final defeat by FC Porto.

Henrik proved when he left Celtic for Manchester United and Barcelona that he could do it at the very top level. Imagine achieving that after all that he did at our club. He showed his class when he returned with Barca and scored against Celtic in the Champions League but refused to celebrate. I always felt it was fitting after all he went through in Seville, after all the work he put in inspiring Celtic to get to that final, that Henrik should taste success in the Champions League final with Barcelona. It was hard for me that it had to be against my old club Arsenal but I was so happy for him that night. It was footballing justice, in my eyes.

He came off the bench to be the architect of Barca's triumph and Thierry Henry said, 'People always talk about Ronaldinho and everything but I didn't see him today – I saw Henrik Larsson. He changed the game, that is what killed the game – sometimes you talk about Ronaldinho and Eto'o and people like that, but you need to talk about the proper footballer who made the difference and that was Henrik Larsson tonight.' In December of that year 2006, Henrik had one last hurrah at the very top as he used Sweden's winter break to enjoy a ten-week stint at Manchester United that helped them to the title and Wayne Rooney to become a better player. Rooney will have learned what I did – that he was in the presence of greatness.

Henrik's place in the Celtic folklore should always be heightened by the fact that he overcame so much to become a legend at the club. By that I mean four different managers in his first three years, as he saw Jansen, Venglos, Barnes and Dalglish come and go. I used to hear all that stuff about how he gave the ball away on his debut and let Chic Charnley in to score for Hibs in a 2-1 defeat for Celtic and how it must have haunted him. I thought, 'Give him a break, he only had one bad game in seven years!' Seriously, I thought the guy was a phenomenon.

He had amazing strength of character to come back from the leg break he had in Lyon before I arrived at the club. I think anyone who looked at the pictures of his leg after that would have been sick to the pits of their stomachs.

If Henrik had stayed at Celtic until he hung up his boots he would have gone past the 300-goal barrier, I'm sure of that. He is stubborn, though; when he made the decision he was leaving he stuck to it despite every heartfelt plea for him to stay. There were fans crying, begging him not go, but he stuck to his guns and took his final bow in an emotional farewell friendly against Seville. Even Henrik cried that day.

I was delighted to see him enjoy his times at United and Barca, because he deserved that. He rose to every occasion for Celtic in the finals and the Old Firm games. The goals in Seville, the chip over Rangers keeper Stefan Klos in that 6-2 derby win. They are all magic memories. The thing is when you were in Henrik's team you genuinely believed that anything could happen when you had him in that line-up. Nine times out ten he produced. If Dalglish's strength was shielding the ball and producing that piece of magic, Henrik's was his unquenchable desire to score goals. I was a little bit in awe of him as a player, to be honest.

Martin O'Neill inherited Henrik as a player but he became a huge fan of him because he knew how pivotal he would be in our success. The year before I came, Celtic won that Treble. Without Larsson I don't think O'Neill would have won that Treble; without Larsson I don't think we would have made that journey to Seville together. He was the catalyst and Martin knew that. He was huge in that side and he so often rescued us. We kept training bubbly for him to get the best out of him. We knew we had a special one amongst us. Henrik, though, had massive respect for the manager and I never once saw him take a liberty with Martin. He was never late, he never shirked training or pushed boundaries in the dressing room by answering back or ridiculing the coaching staff. He could have – by then he was that powerful – but he never did. If it had been Martin O'Neill v Henrik Larsson with the crowd then there would only have been one winner. Larsson. It never happened because there was such respect between them.

Henrik, though, was as powerful an individual player in a football club as I have ever seen. Tony Adams ran the show at Arsenal but George Graham was the Guv'nor. They gelled perfectly like O'Neill and Larsson. If Henrik had wanted to act the arse he could have undermined anything the boss was trying to achieve, but he never showed any signs of trying anything like that.

And the legends we have at Celtic also knew they had something special in their ranks. Jinky loved Henrik because he knew he was quality. I have spoken time and again in this book about the big goals that the big strikers scored. That's exactly what Henrik did.

I look now at the fee that was paid for Henrik and it is a magnificent deal, I mean £650,000 – it is unbelievable when you think about it now. He did everything he had to in his career, he became a god at Celtic, he played for arguably the biggest club in the world in Manchester United and he won the Champions League with Barcelona. Any modern-day kid would see Henrik Larsson as the Greatest Ever Celtic Player because these kids never saw Jimmy Johnstone. Henrik has a claim on that title, it might cause a thousand pub arguments, but in my eyes he was that good.

I know the media didn't like interviewing Henrik too much, he wasn't the joker in the pack and he could be guarded, he didn't jump up and down on chairs at Christmas parties the way I did, but that just wasn't Henrik. It wasn't his personality and why should he try and be something he is not? He was reserved and I would never dream of taking the mickey out of him, he was the top dog in that dressing room, 'Mr Celtic' in our eyes. I walked out as number 10 for Celtic with Henrik as number 7 and those were the best days of my career, looking back now.

I can look back and say that I played with the great Henrik Larsson and that when we went to Ibrox together we didn't travel there in fear – we fancied ourselves to do a job on them. Henrik and I RAN off the bus at Ibrox. Henrik knew Craig Moore was hunting for him, desperate to clatter him and he would jog off the bus ready for it. That was our mind-set. Forget that Premiership thing where they slouch off the bus with their headphones on, we made sure we went off the bus looking like we were delivering a message of intent. Let's get in there, get the job done and get the hell out of this place. That was us, and in Larsson we had the player to set the tone.

Ibrox is where you discover what you have around you as a Celtic player, what they have inside of them. That place will test you to the hilt. Time and again Henrik was up to the test. His seven years in Scottish football should be treasured by every fan who saw him play, as should his fifteen Old Firm goals. We were the best team since the Lisbon Lions and he was our jewel, so I will always bless the day I went to Celtic to have the time of my life beside a legend. Watch any montage of his goals and you will see a gracious side to the man, he always makes a point of running to the guy who provided the pass or the cross for him to feed on. So I don't really care about the way others perceive him, I know the Henrik Larsson I went to work with, and he was a player I am proud to have called my team-mate.

He played for the two biggest clubs in the world in Manchester United and Barcelona, and he was an icon at the third in Celtic, as far as I am concerned. That's why Henrik Larsson is in my Celtic Dream Team.

12

THE BEST I PLAYED WITH

NEVILLE SOUTHALL

LEE DIXON   TONY ADAMS   JOHAN MJALLBY   GARY SPEED
            (captain)

LUBOMIR MORAVČIK   ROY KEANE   RYAN GIGGS

DENNIS BERGKAMP

IAN RUSH   HENRIK LARSSON

I grew up on a tough council estate in Swansea called Trallwn and in those childhood days that were domi-nated by football from dawn to dusk, I wanted to be Ian Rush. I lived there with my brother, two sisters and my parents in a three-bedroom house, and James and I had bunk beds and shared so many laughs. It was a happy house, apart from in the mornings when my old man would be screaming at my sisters not to use all the hot water.

It's a rougher place now than when I was there and a little more rundown, but I never saw it in that light anyway to be honest. I thought it was a great community and my abiding memory is every family being out in the street at New Year linking hands and celebrating when it struck midnight. I didn't feel threatened there, I was just an ordinary kid growing up and dreaming of becoming the next Rushie and making it as a footballer.

My mum would leave £15 in a jar on top of the telly on a Monday and that was £1 a day for the three of us going to school (my youngest sister Victoria is seven years younger than me so wasn't going to school then). I spent it all at the newsagents before I got on the bus, but I was happy with that and I yearned for the freedom of being on the park and scoring goals. I look now at the kids in the game or even just growing up on their X-boxes and all the rest and think the ones who dedicate themselves to football have to have a little bit of steel inside them to ignore all the other distractions, to keep training and trying to make themselves better. Back then I didn't have much other than my football and it didn't bother me one bit.

My first set of boots is in a case at my mum and dad's house now. They were black and yellow and my Nana Hartson bought them for me. She's gone now, bless her, but she must have seen something in me at the age of three and decided I needed boots to get out there and kick the ball about with. The boots came with a Leeds United kit I had and I never had any of the fancy makes until I got a pair of Patrick Kings like Kevin Keegan had. So, unlike some players, I really valued the sports deals I had with Umbro at Arsenal and then with Puma during my five years at Celtic.

I always loved Puma boots and they were loyal to me for over a decade, which was great because I had all my family kitted out in Puma gear. I used to look at it all and think back to those days when my Patricks meant so much to me and have a rueful smile.

I once came on for Rushie in a friendly against Turkey and it felt surreal but I was being brought into that environment to eventually be the player who might try to replace him. An impossible task. I couldn't be the next Ian Rush for Wales, I had to concentrate on being the first John Hartson. I was in awe of that man, for a start. This was the guy who played number 9 for Liverpool and Wales and later in his career for Juventus. When I first met him at international camps, it was quite intimidating.

I was only a teenager when I first got called up from the Under-21s to be in amongst those boys in the senior squad. They knew full well that I wouldn't play but it was felt that I could go to school in that company. Learn my trade as a striker. I couldn't have had a better teacher than Rushie, he was the sole reason I was a Liverpool supporter from a very young age, so to actually be on the same training pitch as him was mind-numbing for me. I remember in June 1991 when we played host to the World Cup holders West Germany and Rushie scored the winner in an unbelievable 1-0 win. That goal summed him up. He had the awareness to play on the shoulder of the German centre-half Guido Buchwald and when the ball was arrowed from the back by Paul Bodin, Rush was on to it in a flash and had the strength to hold off his marker and blast the ball home.

He scored twenty-eight goals in his seventy-three caps for Wales but, like myself, Gary Speed and Ryan Giggs in our generation, he never made it to a major final, which is a crying shame for a striker of that calibre. He was my idol, I was a sixteen-year-old kid making my way at

Luton Town and I just looked at this guy toppling the world champions and loved everything about him as a footballer. He was all that I wanted to be, a different type of player with his pace and nimble play, whereas I was a traditional British rough-house centre-forward, with a bit of ability, I like to think. That didn't stop me hero-worshipping the guy, though. I just thought he was brilliant.

He's still Liverpool's all-time top scorer with 346 goals in his two spells at Anfield, and that's why even if our time together was fleeting on the pitch, I trained enough with Rushie to count him as someone I played with. He taught me so much.

If Rush was an education as a player, then Tony Adams has been such a lesson to me as a person. I played under him at Arsenal and there is only one man to wear my armband in the Best Team I Played With. Adams led men like he was born for the task – so did Roy Keane, but Tony was the one I had the most experience of.

I see him as an inspiration. He saw the inside of a jail cell because of his drinking after he smashed his car into a wall after one session. He was battling demons and, in my eyes, he showed so much bravery in turning his life around. I used the example of my old captain when I had to look myself in the mirror and admit that I was addicted to gambling. I remembered his book – simply called *Addicted* – and how it made me feel when he laid bare just how low he had sunk with the drink. I drew on that and the day I got my one-year pin from Gamblers Anonymous earlier this year, I said a little thank you to Tony and the help his story had been for me. I don't even buy a raffle ticket these days, and it was something I had to face, like Tony did with his alcoholism. Like him, I have found that when you start living your life in a better way then doors start opening for you. Tony started his Sporting Chance charity and after my fight with cancer I built up the John Hartson Foundation.

I don't think I would be in a position to be an assistant coach with Wales now if I hadn't sorted my life out, and my old Arsenal captain played a big role in that just by being an example to me of what you can achieve. I lost so much money to gambling and hit a low point after I had retired from football, and when the money started dribbling away so did some of the so-called friends. Now I have faced up to what I was. I can't change the mistakes I have made in the past, but I can try to make amends for them and I have good people around me to help me do that. It takes courage to be honest with yourself like that and I first saw that kind of bravery the day Tony Adams stood in front of us in the Arsenal dressing room and said, 'Lads, I am alcoholic and I am going to need your help.'

We were all stunned, he was an everyday boozer but we saw that as part of the Adams' character – we never stopped to think how much damage he was doing to himself. The Tony I knew back then was harum-scarum and all over the place off the field, but you could depend on him every time when the chips were down on the pitch. The man I know now is a more balanced person.

Football dressing rooms are unforgiving places, but Tony was a man's man and he had dragged us out of enough holes on the field at Arsenal. He knew he could depend on us and I hope as team-mates we helped a little. In the end, though, it has been his own courage that has seen him able to rebuild his life, and I feel he deserves huge credit for that.

Through the journey of this book it has been interesting for me to assess what I feel is in the make-up of the footballers that I admire. I need to recognise the traits as a person and a player that mark you out as special, because one day I want to be a manager and I see that quality as vital. One of my choices at centre-half would have to be Johan Mjallby, and he has so many of the attributes I treasure. I played with few braver than the big Swede. Boots would be flying and he would put his head in to get the block in. He could play too and I always felt he brought a lot of midfield experience to his position at the back, having played so much of his career in the engine room.

We used to have fearsome battles on a Friday morning and we didn't even have the usual excuses for those confrontations. Normally. I'd see those bitter clashes start in training when it was a guy who had the hump with the other player because one was in the side and one wasn't. So you get what I would always call the Friday Morning Barney.

Not Johan and me though. We were both starters in the Martin O'Neill days at Celtic, so I think we have to be honest and admit that we just loved a scrap! A lot of the time at Celtic Johan was secretly nursing his way through knee trouble so think how good he would have been in the Hoops 100 per cent fit. Mjallby, though, was an excellent choice as Neil Lennon's lieutenant. I would be critical of the signings of some of the foreign players Celtic have brought in at times but never of Johan or of Lubomir Moravčik.

Lubo was in the twilight of his career when we joined forces at Celtic, but he was still an unbelievable talent. He could whip in an in-swinger with either foot and he was so two-footed you literally couldn't tell which was his stronger foot. Some of the things he could do with the ball in training I had just never seen before. There was one day in the middle of a training game at Barrowfield when we were careering around trying to impress the gaffer and the ball went about forty feet in the air. Lubo proceeded to trap it stone dead with his ARSE. It's true. I mean he squatted down and it bounced up and he killed it stone dead.

He was like Mark Hughes on the training field in that respect. I remember being in the middle of one Welsh session and Dean Saunders and I were marvelling at the work of Mark Hughes. Sparky was brilliant, even balls fired in at a bad height were no problem. He was so supple he would just launch himself into a position and thrash home a volley. Deano turned to him at the end of the session and said, 'Is there anything you can't ****ing do?' He could volley, head it so well, he could do everything.

Because of his age and all the demands placed upon us, Martin couldn't always play Lubo, but he trusted him implicitly as a footballer. There were few better players on free-kicks than Lubo and I think he was always a top-class operator in the game. We may have discovered Moravčik late in his career but in the French League they already knew what they had. He was a phenomenal player in France and last summer you saw Luka Modric quit Spurs for Real Madrid in a £27.5 million deal, which made me wonder what Moravčik would be worth in the market now.

I'll never forget when we came back from playing Juventus in the Stadio delle Alpi when we had lost 3-2 in the Champions League and I had Pavel Nedved's shirt. We were robbed by a dodgy penalty that night – we'd gain revenge winning 4-3 at our place, inspired by Sutty – but when we got back home the disappointment was fading a little and I could reflect on swapping jerseys with Pavel Nedved.

When we arrived back I decided to give Lubo the Nedved shirt and you could see it meant a lot to him to have it – he was his hero and I'm glad it lives with him now. The rest of my shirts are running round Swansea playing Sunday League football. I gave them all away – even the Vieri and the Costacurta ones!

Men like Mjallby, Keane, Moravčik and Larrson were all by my side when we played together in some of the great arenas of the world. On my travels there were some special ones, but it would be impossible to beat Celtic Park. It truly is my favourite because, especially on European nights, the place just rocks.

As a boyhood Liverpool fan going to Anfield was always going to mean so much to me when I made it to play on that stage. The hairs on the back of your neck stand up when you see that sign in front of you: 'This is Anfield'. You go down steps and it is upwards to the pitch. Anfield is on your eye-line then and you know that when you emerge it will be mayhem and you are in one of the great cathedrals of football.

Highbury meant a lot to me in my Arsenal days and the surface was always like a bowling green there, the groundsman had a cupboard full of awards. Abroad I have played in all the ones I wanted to visit. I played and scored in the Nou Camp when Celtic drew 1-1 with Barcelona, sampled the San Siro and lost a European Super Cup final 2-0 there to AC Milan in my Gunners days. I played at Bayern Munich, scored at Old Trafford twice for Coventry City against Manchester United, and Andy Goram was in goal!

If there were two grounds I wished I'd scored at it would be White Hart Lane for Arsenal against Spurs and Tynecastle for Celtic. I had the complete set in the SPL, apart from away to Hearts and it bugged me. I hit the bar, the lot, but just couldn't get a goal there.

I scored enough, though, to hang up my boots feeling I had fulfilled the dreams I had growing up in Trallwn. I wasn't the next Rushie but I am proud of both what I achieved and the list of men I got to call my friends and team-mates.

13

THE BEST I PLAYED AGAINST

TIM FLOWERS

CAFU   MARTIN KEOWN   ROBERTO AYALA   PAOLO MALDINI

MARCEL DESAILLY   BRYAN ROBSON

CRISTIANO RONALDO   RONALDINHO

WAYNE ROONEY   THIERRY HENRY

It's only now that I can properly look back in wonder at some of the stars I played against in my football career; when I had my boots on I was intent on smashing them about the place and scoring goals. That's the truth of the matter. As a footballer I would always respect the players I faced but I let a lot of the pomp of the occasions we shared pass me by because I didn't care too much for these players. My mind-set was that I couldn't because I had to win. Simple as that.

I was hungry and passionate, I had come from the streets of Swansea and this was my passport to the life I wanted. I carried anger inside of me all the time, I wanted to make my mark in this world. My dad always said to me, 'Show these men every respect in the world off the pitch and when you are sharing a beer in the Players Lounge afterwards. But when you cross that white line, John, as far as I am concerned, it is dog eat dog and you do what you have to do to win. This is a cruel game you are going into. You get nothing for being nice.'

I look up to my old man, always have. So I always lived by those words, but now life is very different for me. I make my living analysing what these players do and I had a little laugh to myself recently when I was doing some media work to discuss the shock £24 million departure of Dutch striker Robin van Persie from my old club Arsenal to Manchester United. These days I can't take my eyes off RVP and ten years ago I wouldn't have given him the time of day! One day I will be able to tell my son Joni about playing against the likes of Paolo Maldini and all the great grounds I have scored at, from Old Trafford to the Nou Camp, but when it was actually happening to me it was past me in a flash.

Throughout this book I have tried to weave the stories of those I have played with and against into the chapters of the Celtic heroes I have chosen in my Dream Team. Looking back on it, I could have picked THREE teams of the stars that I have played against. I know, for instance, that people will point to the fact that I faced Gianluigi Buffon, the Italian legend, but I have picked Tim Flowers as the best I've played against. The thing is, I have always respected players who work so hard to get every shred out of themselves, and Tim was like that. So were a lot of players in the Blackburn Rovers side he played in that won the Premier League title under Kenny Dalglish and which also had the SAS partnership of Alan Shearer and Chris Sutton up front.

Flowers defied everything that Ian Wright and I could throw at him that night I have talked about at Ewood Park. It was ridiculous and I remember shaking his hand at the end and telling him, 'We have just lost 1-0 and we would have won this game 6-1 if it wasn't for you. You've just had the game of your life, Tim.' I have never seen a goalkeeper turn in ninety minutes like he did that night and that's why I gave him the nod here because even now it sticks in my mind. Yes, I've probably played against better keepers in Buffon and Victor Valdes against Barcelona, but I've given it to Tim because I have never forgiven him for that night.

At centre-half Martin Keown would hurt you without even trying to hurt you. He was so bony and gangly with his elbows, he didn't even know himself what part of him he was hitting you with. He loved being physical and he was like me in that football was a release for him, the place where he liked to let off some steam.

I don't think Celtic really saw the beast John Hartson could be, the one that English football saw a lot of. And there was a reason for that. Martin O'Neill didn't drain the aggression out of me as such but what he did was that he reminded me of the importance of discipline, a message that came from his days with Brian Clough when he worked under him at Nottingham Forest. Martin always told me that Cloughie hated ill discipline and he drummed it into them that every booking would be frowned upon.

I only had two red cards in five years at Celtic, both of which I earned in my first season in Scottish football. The first one was stupidity when I kicked out at Aberdeen's Jamie McAllister in a game we already had won at 2-0 with just five minutes left. That was idiotic when I think back on it and now that I am a coach with Wales I can see how managers get so upset with players when they do things like that. So Martin wanted to drag all that out of me. I became a more rounded, better player for the lessons I learned on how to temper my aggression. So Celtic fans never saw me at my most evil because of Martin! He made me tune in and control myself and I tell players now when I am coaching that they need to be in control of their aggression and not let it take charge of them. It's like ice and fire, that's what you need inside of you. Ice water in your veins and a fire burning in your soul. That's the best way to describe how a footballer should operate at the very top level.

One guy who had that when I played against him was the French international midfielder Marcel Desailly. He was in the AC Milan side when Arsenal lost the European Super Cup 2-0 to them over two legs in 1995. Desailly was a rock for them at the heart of midfield, just as he would be later in his career at Chelsea.

When people talk to me about the feeling of desolation when I missed out on the UEFA Cup final in Seville through my back injury, I nod and agree with them because it was devastating at the time for me. But on reflection over my entire career I have to acknowledge that some players go through their days without ever sniffing a major Euro final and I played in TWO. The Celtic fans often forget that.

I played and scored in the 2-1 European Cup Winners' Cup final against Real Zaragoza in the Parc des Princes and the moment when Paul Merson cut it back to me and I got there to sweep the ball home across the keeper and into the far corner will always live with me. I was just a twenty-year-old kid and it could have been the career-defining goal for me. That strike made the score on the night 1-1 and I'd be lying if I didn't say that at the time for a fleeting moment I dreamed it was going to go down in the Gunners' history books as the bedrock of a comeback win for us. Sadly, Nayim decided to try a shot from nearly the halfway line and the rest is a YouTube moment that I hate seeing even now.

I was such a young player then but I was trusted in the quarter-final against Auxerre and in both legs of the semi-final against Sampdoria when I stuck my penalty away in a nerve-shredding shootout. The way Zaragoza won that night was bad enough but to do it with almost the last kick of the ball was just horrible. If I close my eyes I can still see Nayim's shot from way out on the touchline swirling over David's head. He actually back-pedalled well to get to the flight of the shot but then fatally he mistimed his jump and didn't get enough on it and the ball fell into the net with David slumped in misery. I could only look back in disbelief. What an awful feeling it was to lose a final like that.

Before that I had played in the European Super Cup final against AC Milan because Arsenal won the Cup Winners' Cup in 1994 against Parma and earned the right to face the European Cup holders of AC Milan.

In Paris that night against Zaragoza they kept me on because the extra-time was ebbing away from us and I had scored in the semi-final shootout. Then Nayim came up with that one flash of brilliance and it was all snatched away from us. The goal I scored that night in Paris will always live with me but the truth is that we lost the match and I came to look upon that twenty-five-yarder I scored in Celtic's win over Liverpool on the road to Seville as the best of my life. They're all glory days stories now, things to reflect upon when I am having a pint or a round of golf with my mates. I have had my day as a footballer now.

Much as it would alarm the likes of Harry Redknapp and Martin O'Neill, who had to nurse me through pre-season and try to get me back down to my fighting weight at times, I would love the chance now to cut my teeth as a head coach one day. John Hartson the manager will be a mixture of all the styles I have learned, I think. If there is a ball to be played over the top, my teams will play it. If you have a quick striker then use him. Equally, I like to see teams get the ball down and play and I think Barcelona have set a precedent now that makes every coach think of how they should work. They have shown you can be 5'6'' and beat the world the way Xavi, Lionel Messi and Andres Iniesta have.

There is still a place for a big centre-forward in football. I have to think that guys like me or a different big guy, like Peter Crouch, has a future. I think of all the different types of player and I yearn for the day when I will be in the dugout ready to stand on my own two feet and find my own management style. I have loved watching Brendan Rogers stamp his mark all over my team Swansea City and earn himself the Liverpool job. There can't be much wrong with the way he sets up his teams. Flat back four, two full-backs pushing on, deep-lying midfielder, two wide intelligent players and a striker who has to graft for the system. Swansea went to Anfield and monopolised possession. I looked at them that night and thought I would love my team to play like that.

If you study anyone over the last two years, study my team Swansea, they were up there at fifth in the European passing stats with the Barcelonas and the Real Madrids, and that's down to Brendan Rogers. So I would have a mix of that and the man-management of the gaffer, Martin O'Neill. I never knew where I was with him – I still don't, but I think it is right that there should be a distance between manager and player. You can't be best friends with a player because you will have to drop him one day, you have to have a little bit of a fear factor there. José Mourinho, Sir Alex Ferguson – they will both tell you they are still learning about this game. Me? As a coach I have only just started, I learned more about preparation and coaching in my first four days in the Welsh backroom staff than I had in ten years as a player.

The next chapter of my football life is about to unfold and after all I have been through, beating cancer and battling back from the brink, just tugging my boots on and getting back on a training pitch feels so good. I'm ready for the battle.

14

THE TEAM OF MY DREAMS

When you pick a Celtic Dream Team you have to be mindful that this is not just any old football club, this is a place with heritage, with 125 years of rich history to draw on, with a way of playing that the fans love. That was always in my mind when I came up with the team below:

SIMPSON

MCGRAIN   AITKEN   MCNEILL   GEMMELL
(captain)

JOHNSTONE   MURDOCH   MCSTAY   LENNOX

DALGLISH   LARSSON

It's been a journey to come down to that eleven and I think it is fascinating to look at the men I have chosen and think how they would have melded together as a team. I think when you look at my side you can't dispute the strength running through its core, the athleticism and brilliance wide and the sheer striking venom up front.

In the days when Danny McGrain and Tommy Gemmell played there were some swashbuckling players in their positions but you would also have so many of them sitting in to defend their zones. Those guys refused to settle for that. They played with a spirit of adventure and they would have fitted like a glove in the modern game where the full-backs are all great athletes who push right up the pitch and almost play like wingers. Look at the likes of Dani Alves at Barcelona. McGrain and Gemmell were from that mould and you only have to look at how far up the field Tommy was when he scored that famous goal in Lisbon to see testimony of that. McGrain was also renowned for charging on and that's why I picked them as a partnership in the wide areas.

I think it's great to see echoes of the past in the current Celtic team that Neil Lennon is constructing. Adam Matthews and Emilio Izaguirre are very attack-minded players and they like to be a threat for us. They are paying homage to McGrain and Gemmell, in my eyes.

In Roy Aitken and Billy McNeill you have such experience and knowledge as a combination of centre-halves. I think people will debate the selection of big Roy, but I look at the two of them and think they were just defensive monsters. Both could head the ball, they could play on the deck and they could lead people. Aitken earned so many caps for Scotland in midfield and like Johan Mjallby – who almost got the nod for my side and who I loved playing with – he brought a midfielder's passing range to the heart of defence. This game we all love is about opinions and to my mind Aitken was simply a tower of a man who brought bravery and strength to the position. He was the type of stopper I loved to play against because I knew you could have an honest battle with men like him.

The back four I have selected are rock-solid and I would give the full-backs the licence to go forward if I could dislodge Jock Stein for a day and be the Dream Team manager.

The players I have picked give you so many options in formation if you look at them. With my job with Wales now I love to study the ways you can set up with players of ability. I mean, if you went 4-1-2-3 or 4-3-3 you would have Dalglish and Lennox either side of Larsson. Can you imagine that? Frightening.

Personally, I think we should maybe simplify this and go 4-4-2, with Lennox playing like Georgios Samaras does often for the current team. Yes, he would be playing off the left but he would be allowed to go in and join Henrik and Kenny whenever he liked because he was so forward-thinking. Lennox's unbelievable goal return gives you so much threat coming in off the left and he was such a clever footballer that he would understand the job and do his defensive duties for the team too. On the right side you just let Jinky do whatever he wants because he is a genius!

So 4-4-2 or we go fluid and into a 4-3-3 – whatever way you look at it, I think it is a phenomenal team. I have put a lot of thought into the players I have selected in the book and I ended up with all these balls of paper in the bin in my office because I kept picking teams and then thinking of another player I could go for.

Look at the goals in the side from Lennox to Dalglish and Larsson. The goal tally in the Hoops of those three is just awesome and that was a big factor in my thinking with them.

There could be only one captain, as I have said, and it would have to be Cesar. There are many men who have

worn the armband in my Dream Team – McGrain, Aitken, McStay – but I feel Billy sticks out. The ultimate
leader.

Listen, I know I am going to sit with the punters now
when I meet them at functions and they will argue with
me over who I have picked here. I think, though, that
middle to front you can't argue with those six players.
Goalkeepers, full-backs and a centre-half beside big Billy
you can have the debates about for me. In the Afterword
to this book, for instance, you will discover that current
Celtic boss Neil Lennon doesn't agree with my eleven. Big
shock there then!

Seriously, there are some who are musts and then the
arguments start to rage. I just think some of the players I
have are a different breed. I have left great players out
who I really rate. Men like Paolo di Canio and Paul
Lambert. I can only pick eleven players, however, and
if there is one I am delighted to hail in these pages it is
Paul McStay, for his courage in staying with the club
when they were going through some dismal times. He
gave people a reason to go to the football on a Saturday
when we were toiling as a club and I think that is the
mark of a true Celtic man.

I would love to watch my Dream Team, just for ninety
minutes to see if I have got the blend right. This is like an
episode of Fantasy Football but from here on in I am
praying that my life will be about this, assembling squads
then finding the right starting eleven. My coaching role
with Wales right now is invaluable because I am educating myself to become a manager. You think you know the
game as a player and then you come into an international
camp and see the level of preparation that goes into one

World Cup qualifier from the coaches. It's staggering. The reason there is that if you map out the day correctly, give the players the drills and the information they need, it can all give you that vital edge at the very top level. I am loving the involvement and I am developing as a football man.

This has been such a fun project to be involved in and I think I have loved it because I look at every exercise now and imagine picking a team to win on a Saturday. It has been a real eye-opener for me because I am honest enough to admit that I wasn't always the best professional – even at Celtic, where I would average over twenty goals a season.

If I am honest, I grew up as a footballer in a drinking culture and I realise that now. I remember turning up for camps with the Welsh squad and the first day and a half was spent in the bar! We would socialise together – myself, Gary Speed and the present gaffer, Chris Coleman. Those were different times. Now our camps are completely dry, not a drink is taken. I drank too much, ate too much and stayed up too late too often when I was a player. Now I look at this era and know I must adapt to what is now demanded of football people.

I believe that in any football environment the manager sets the tone and that's why Jock Stein would have been the perfect man to control my eleven from Heaven. You lead by example now and players watch you to see that your level of ambition matches theirs. They don't want you to be sitting up having five pints in the hotel bar before bed – they want you to be as dedicated as they are.

I want to be the best manager I can be and I am going back to school in the game I grew up in. I am learning the systems piece by piece and I have taken in more these past six months as a Wales coach than I did in the last fifteen years as a player. That's the truth, you live in a bubble as a top footballer these days. You worry about yourself, your performances, your place in the team. Now I have to grow up and use every shred of experience I get in Wales' World Cup campaign.

When I hung up my boots I used to think that I could walk into a manager's job at a club but I was kidding myself on. I would have been nowhere near ready then, and I am not ready now, but I will be. I operated at the top level as a striker but that is no guarantee to me becoming a top manager. There are some great managers like Jock Stein, Sir Alex Ferguson, Walter Smith, José Mourinho and Brendan Rodgers, who by their own admissions were not the greatest of players. They have the Midas touch as bosses, though, and that's what you have to try to capture. I have played for the likes of Arsene Wenger, for instance. Training at Arsenal under Arsene was done to a stopwatch. If he said we were spending eight minutes on shooting then we were spending eight minutes and not eight minutes and twenty-five seconds, or he lost the plot! Then I worked with Harry Redknapp, who was more laid-back, and Martin O'Neill, who saved all of his intensity for match day. They all did it differently and I will try to take a piece from each of them because they are legends.

I hope to use the grounding I have to become a top-drawer boss and I have every confidence that I can do that. I am on the right path. For now that means helping my country, and I have looked at how people like Dean Saunders have used their time as coaches as learning spells in their life. Deano worked with Graeme Souness and soaked so much in. Steve Clarke has to have absorbed a mountain of knowledge when he was Mourinho's right-hand man at Chelsea. Now he has the hot-seat at West Bromwich Albion and has earned huge respect.

These guys are the templates for me – I know that's what I must do. I will manage one day – I just pray that when the chance comes I get to be in charge of a side half as good as my Celtic Dream Team!

AFTERWORD
BY NEIL LENNON
Manager, Celtic Football Club

When Iain King came into Lennoxtown to do the interview for this book, it was August 31, 2012. Transfer deadline day, and he wanted to talk about the Celtic Dream Team? I was sat in my office at my work trying to build one! Seriously, that day ended with the likes of strikers Miku and Lassad coming into the club from La Liga, and along with Nigerian defender Efe Ambrose they will get their own chance to become heroes in a place that John Hartson and I loved so much.

The great thing about projects like this Celtic Dream Team is that it makes you sit down and realise just how many truly great players have worn the Hoops. I always felt that every game I played in that famous jersey was an honour, and I have to be honest and admit that when I left Celtic for Nottingham Forest I just couldn't feel the same buzz playing my football with another club.

Looking through John's team intrigued me and given the odd barney we had on the pitch I don't think it would surprise him to find that I disagree with his selection. Mind you, it's only on two positions. I think middle to front of John's Dream Team there are cases that you simply can't argue. I agreed with his midfield four and I think the front two are picks. Can you see past Dalglish and Larsson? Only Mr McGrory could have split that partnership, but in the modern era I think you naturally edge towards those you saw playing.

As a Celtic-player-turned-coach-turned-manager, the chance to select my own Celtic Dream Team was too good to miss. So here goes. This is my Heaven's Eleven.

Goalkeeper:
ARTUR BORUC

I know a lot of people would go for the Lisbon Lions keeper Ronnie Simpson and I understand that logic, but it would have be Artur for me, and I would say right now that our big fella Fraser Forster at the moment is not far behind him. Artur was just so clean in everything he did and he was fantastically agile and great with both feet. He was some keeper and he made really important saves in big games. He had a terrific temperament, and you need that at this club.

Defence:
DANNY McGRAIN

He is a legend and he was world class as a right-back. A real attacking force and I would have to say a player before his time in that respect. He redefined the position he played in.

JOHAN MJALLBY

John Clark was, from what I have seen on tape and the stories I have heard inside the club, the perfect foil around the next guy I would always have as one of my centre-halves. But I have to have faith with my number 2 here, and Johan was such a superb defender for the club. Brave as a lion, and he could play a bit too.

BILLY McNEILL

He's the man who lifted the European Cup, the first British player to do so, and he was just a commanding presence in central defence. A lock-in for this position for me.

TOMMY GEMMELL

Scored in two separate European Cup finals and so many people forget his strike against Feyenoord in 1970 because we lost that final, and the winner against Inter Milan in Lisbon in 1967 meant so much to the club. Again he gave you an added dimension at left-back because he was such a threat going forward.

Midfield:
JIMMY JOHNSTONE

The Greatest Ever Celt and I think his dribbling ability, his creativity and the desire to entertain the Celtic fans summed up the heart and the soul of our club.

PAUL McSTAY

He was in my era as a Celtic supporter and he was a real stand-out in a poor team at the time. He was a million miles ahead of others, and I always remember watching him at Euro 92 alongside the likes of Gary McAllister and Stuart McCall and thinking he was one of the best players in the entire tournament.

BOBBY MURDOCH

Another player who I can only see in fleeting glimpses on tape, but the stories they tell you inside Celtic are of an exquisite footballer. I think you could have looked at Bertie Auld or others in this position, but Murdoch would get my nod.

BOBBY LENNOX

Pace, desire and Celtic's second all-time scorer behind James McGrory and ahead of Henrik Larsson. Enough said.

Forwards:
KENNY DALGLISH

He was my hero as a kid – I just loved everything about the way he played his football at Liverpool and the great goals he scored.

HENRIK LARSSON

This might sound like an odd term for a team-mate, but Henrik was also my hero. He was an icon to the fans but to those of us who played with him? We loved the guy because he was a superstar yet he was down-to-earth with us and a great team-mate. He had so much media attention around him constantly and he scored the big goals when we really needed them. I can remember when he was at Barcelona that Samuel Eto'o had been scoring every week and then he disappeared to the African

Nations Cup. There was huge pressure for Henrik to then come in and fill his boots, but he did what he does and he scored every week. That summed him up, he got better and better as his career went on and his mentality was fantastic. He was one of those players who had complete faith in his own ability. Some people mistake that for arrogance with Henrik but it's not, he just knew what he could bring to the table. I think it is natural I should use him as an example to the younger players at Celtic today. I mean, he came in to train with us one day and we beat Aberdeen 9-0 on the Saturday and I told him to come in every week! I wish . . .

Neil Lennon
Lennoxtown
September 2012